Go See the Kids

Lizzie Harwood

Go See the Kids

Cover design by Editor Deluxe
Author photo by sarahgardan.com

Published by Editor Deluxe Press

Dedication

For Béatrice and Vivienne,
two honey-bunnies

One

Leo drove them to Pierre Trudeau Airport, on the outskirts of Montreal, their closest hub. On the Quebec highway he steered with his knees on purpose to scare Faye.

"Do I really have to check on Nadine?" he repeated. "How often?"

"She's your sister. Be reasonable, kiddo," Faye said.

"Why don't you just put her in a loony bin?"

"She's not quite loony enough," Richard answered, "in fact, she's not loony at all when a social worker visits."

"Maybe she's just allergic to family," Leo said under his breath.

"What are you so mad about, kiddo?" Faye started to feel carsick, she had to talk to outpace the nausea. "You've got the house to yourself for you and your pals. The rent's paid. What's the big sour face for? You just have to go check on Nadine now and then. She gets lonely without Sienna here. She likes to see you."

"Yeah, and try to save me. All she talks about is Jesus-this and Jesus-that."

They pulled up to the airport drop-off zone.

"Nadine's only religious because of that bout of measles that went round in the early sixties. She almost died. I'm sure she developed temporal lobe disturbance from it. I saw a show about it. It makes them hallucinate and go all religious."

Leo filled a cart with their small bags of luggage and wheeled them inside.

"Sure, Mom. It's nothing to do with

you and Dad's genes, eh?"

"It's a little known theory. It's still being researched."

Inside the airport, Richard wandered off immediately. Faye only realized this when she and Leo were almost at the head of the queue and she turned to her husband for a pen.

"O where in the world is that man?"

It was best, Faye believed, to roll up at an airport four hours before any flight. That way, in her dark gray pantsuit with her hair set overnight into curls and lips adorned with coral lipstick, she usually received a free upgrade to business class. Richard's appearance didn't exactly help, but there was something in his demeanor, an innocence in the gray tufts decorating his ears, or a frailty in his tweed suit that was old enough to vote that ensured Richard got upgraded also.

They usually never traveled

together. The kids used to ask why and Faye said, "In case the plane goes down. So you won't be orphaned. The British Royal Family does the same." But that was a little white lie: it was always due to airfares. They went for the bargains and rarely booked the same day. Plus, Faye preferred to fly without Richard.

This trip, the Ventures couple *had* to travel as a duo. Faye viewed this as a bad omen. Her nerves were frazzled. She'd spent all of Christmas afternoon round at Nadine's waiting for her to show up so she could give her forgotten-by-the-tree presents. Nadine appeared at nine o'clock at night saying a friend had a crisis and she had healed him of his woes.

Faye had stayed up half the night packing and running panicky thoughts around her brain like a marathon competitor. That morning, she rang Nadine to say goodbye and tried to tell her she loved her but it came out as: "I want you to promise to eat more meat, okay?"

"Damn him, where's he gone to now?"

Faye and Leo craned their necks, scanning the low-ceilinged hangar for tell-tale flashes of Richard's ample silver hair. No trace of crinkly blue eyes set in a face of smile lines. Not a whisper of his ambling gait that seemed off-kilter but covered ground fast for an octogenarian. Faye's heart beat in triplicate. They were one person away from the check-in counter. He had to be here. What if he'd fallen somewhere? He was likely to be outside, watching how the parking meters ticked, or to be in some Personnel-Only area, gauging how many pieces of luggage per conveyor belt could be ferried. Damn him. He made her so scared with this fake senility.

"Quick, Leo, go check around. Run!"

Leo took off, his legs eating up the russet carpet tiles. He lapped around United Airlines, Continental, Canadian Pacific, British Airways, disappearing from view.

The girl at the counter signaled to Faye. She shuffled forward, straining to place each tiny bag on the scales. Each looked deceptively feather-weight, but every one weighed a ton, with paraphernalia vacuum-packed into every nook and cranny. Faye's handbag, casually hanging off her shoulder, was the heaviest item of all. "What you got in there," Leo complained when he'd tried to lift it. "Bricks or the Crown Jewels?"

"Both." Of course it was both.

Faye carried around junk, she realized, and things that were more precious than God. Junk was the stuff she needed. Motion sickness pills, lipstick, her World Clock Calculator, leather address book and a hefty murder to read. The Jewels were items she wanted to take for her children. Little things she thought they'd need in their lives now. Not presents. Old, almost lost things. A book for Junie on watercolor techniques, photos of Will aged three months and newspaper clippings about children's book writers, the last letter written by Sienna's tragic father before he died (saved from Nadine's garbage can), Matt's extracted wisdom teeth found in the bathroom cupboard. Ingrid and Skye's childhood development books. Where was that stupid man?

The girl studied the tickets. She had bouffant auburn hair, small hoop earrings, and bright pink lipstick that clashed with the red-and-white Air

Canada uniform.

"Checking in to Vancouver today, Ma'am?"

"Not stopping in Vancouver, it's transit, we're going on to Auckland via Honolulu," Faye replied, smiling faintly. Ready to collapse on the awful carpet. Twisting her neck to see if Leo had retrieved that idiot of a husband.

"Wow, that's a long trip. You folks been there before? I always wanted to get to New Zealand, but wow, that's like twenty-something hours, eh?"

She tapped the keyboard like an excited Labrador digging for treasure.

"We used to live there. It is a long way. We're visiting our children. My husband is... he's just in the restroom."

Leo appeared, trailing Richard like slipstream, wildness in their eyes.

"I was only changing some money,"

Richard explained. He wasn't concerned about missing the check-in. He never was. He'd turn up late to his own funeral.

The girl hardly glanced at Richard's offered passport. Too excited about their destination. "I had a boyfriend from Australia once. But he moved back. I never got a chance to go there, either."

"Well, Australia's a lot hotter than New Zealand," Faye conceded.

The tapping stopped. Richard muttered something about a packet of chewing gum and disappeared again. Leo hovered beside her. He seemed at the point of saying something important. The check-in girl smiled at Faye, a goofy look that made her face almost pretty. Faye considered asking her if she was single, perhaps Leo could ask her out on a date.

"I've got room for you and your

husband in business class," she said, thrilled with her own ingenuity. "You'll be much more comfortable there, for such a long-haul flight. Don't forget to stretch your legs." She handed Faye the boarding passes and tickets with giddy triumph, "You wouldn't want to get Deep Vein Thrombosis!"

Their luggage zoomed beyond view and Faye held onto Leo's elbow urgently, as he steered her past the fray. Richard had nonchalantly taken possession of one of the bench seats near the departure gate. Without a care in the world. His foot tapped out an air drum accompaniment. She could merrily strangle him.

Leo found his mother a seat, "You alright?"

"Yes, yes. Yes."

She was suddenly too frightened to get on the plane. Richard was not to be trusted, she could see that clearly. If only Leo were coming with them.

She thrust the tickets at Richard, near tears, wanting to go home and forget this trip.

"Why did you have to change money right then?" She wanted to say that she'd needed him to think of her sometimes, but wouldn't.

Richard said something about monitoring the exchange rate and it being better to change the American dollar here rather than there. He peered at the boarding passes. "How wonderful, Faye. You got us an upgrade," he squirreled his face into a Mister-Magoo caricature, "But you've got us going all the way to Auckland."

"And?" Faye demanded, her patience had frayed in so many places it lay in tatters around her, whimpering undeclared war.

"We're getting off in Hawaii, remember? What about Junie?"

Damn and blast. Junie would be at

Oahu International, scanning faces, worrying about them. Their oldest child was the first stop. It had slipped her mind.

"O what are we going to do? Our bags are checked straight through to Auckland!" Faye was off, like a greyhound at the gun's crack, nosing her way back to the queue. Leo's head swung on an incredulous pendulum from parent to parent. Dumbstruck.

"God, it's the blind leading the blind," Leo parted the queue and cleared his throat politely in front of the redhead. "Excuse me, but my parents have checked in too far."

Leo argued with the check-in woman reasonably and calmly while Faye held onto Richard's coat sleeve. The lights in the terminal were unrelenting. She flushed pink as the waiting line of strangers heard how she'd mistaken their destination.

"They're supposed to get off in Honolulu to visit my oldest sister. They're going round the world to visit all their kids."

"You mean she forgot the first kid?"

"Well, yes, with my Dad being late and all, she just got confused. They fly to Auckland from Honolulu in a fortnight."

Faye felt the audience scrutinize her for signs of being a neglectful mother. They gaped at the thought of Richard siring seven children. She wanted to slap the nearest tut-tutting smug mother and ask her how would she like to raise all those kids with Richard as a co-parent? How would she like to have lived through several kids near-death experiences? The sheer number took her breath away. These mothers probably got a decent amount of sleep. And had relatives living nearby. Faye could see it on their horrified faces: they would never, ever forget a child.

Big deal.

Leo continued to win over the check-in girl.

"So the bags can be rerouted with only a day's delay? That's swell."

"I'll cancel the penalties. It's still going to be a big trip for them. Are you sure they're up to it?"

The stage-whispering fooled nobody. The line smirked. They'd asked themselves the same question.

"God, yes," Leo laughed. "These two are probably the most competent travelers you could meet. That's been the first confusion in about fifty years of traveling all over. They've got tarmac fatigue they've been down so many runways!"

The girl laughed and winked. They managed to keep their upgrades. Why didn't they have Leo coming? Faye upgraded Leo on her child mantra (she classified each as *so-so, troubled* or *fine*). Leo should really move from *so-so* to *fine*. He was an exceptional child. He'd been stymied by that horrible teacher, Mrs. What'sherface when he started school, that's why he took so long to read. His IQ tests were near genius. Or was that Skye? No, it was Leo. She sometimes had trouble figuring out which child did what. But she never forgot exact figures obtained in IQ tests. Leo had scored 118. She was sure of that.

In 1976 they moved to an island, fifty kilometers off the Auckland mainland, fifty kilometers in length, with no electricity—only generators and windmills. They ran the main general store, which included the telephone exchange, petrol station, gas-bottle filling station, taxi service and they all lived above and behind the shop in an A-frame apartment. The older kids worked behind the counter and the three youngest attended the two-room school down the road and fended for themselves before and after class. Faye worked day and night. The telephone exchange rang in the middle of the night, in the midst of dreams, interrupting dinner, she ran to the switchboard to patch through the locals' calls. She was their link to the outside world.

Leo rushed into her operator booth and tugged on her slacks. She plugged through another call from a local to the mainland. The archaic board was a mass of plugs and cords wrapped in checkered fabric, she'd created a nest of snakes that afternoon with the Friday flurry of calls to and fro. Half the locals' phone conversations were of nothing more than five-cent gossip and backbiting.

"What is it?" she said, unpeeling his soft fingers from the cotton polyester. Another junction rang— Brring! Brring! Bring us out of the dark ages, it said. Leo held up a picture.

"Look what I did!"

"Oh! Isn't that lovely! What a lovely cloud. And that's—what's that? Is that the sky? And this? That's the sea? That's a beautiful painting, Leo. And look, you wrote your name!"

He'd actually written OEL. The forlorn letters loomed large in black over a muddy smear of the heavens and a violent sea in purple. The cloud was the most delicately rendered item to be seen—in silver with flecks of the sky encroaching in a maudlin taupe. Faye gazed at her youngest, his hair a strong Scandinavian blonde, eyes hoping for praise. He breathed in and out deeply, waiting;

he smelled like candy bananas that someone manning the shop counter must've given him. His belly poked through the striped wool sweater she'd knitted. It was the one that she'd accidentally knitted three arms for. He'd asked to keep the unwanted extra woolen arm and slept with it every night. It was probably going to give him asthma.

"That's very good, Leo, you wrote your name and everything." She bent over and kissed the top of his head. He waited for more. But her back hurt from leaning down at such an angle and another phone line flashed urgent red, Brring! Brring! Bring us human contact.

"There's a good boy. You go and play now. Where are the girls?"

"Skye and Ingrid went swimming. They said I can't come."

"Oh, that's too bad. Maybe Will is upstairs? Or you can watch *The*

Wombles."

She checked her watch. Four o'clock. She wouldn't finish until seven. And then even after that, there were still calls to put through, from upstairs in the alcove, for re-opening fees each time.

Leo turned away, in search of somebody, and Faye put his painting beside her cold mug of tea.

The re-issuing of tickets had wasted a lot of time. But that's why Faye always made sure she was at the airport so early. They stood before the departure gate. Leo twisted his car keys in his fingers.

"Alright, then. I guess I'd better go. Say hi to everybody from me."

Richard gave Leo a bear hug, gruffly muttering that he loved him and repeating last-minute advice on the whereabouts of important papers, keys and the mini snowblower in the basement. Richard wiped his eyes with his decrepit handkerchief. It was blue tartan striped with a once-white middle, now gone the color of a thousand washes. He always cried saying goodbye. She couldn't understand him. He stood there and leaked a little, spontaneously.

She stepped forward, "Thanks for bringing us out, and for the tickets. You're a big help. And look in on Nadine, please. She needs company. Be nice to your sister. And don't start feeding any stray damaged cats this time. I can't bear it when they end up dying."

He smiled in a tight line, as if he couldn't wait to get away.

She gripped his shoulder, "Anyway, we'll see you soon."

They moved on. Their passports and paraphernalia were checked. He waved from the rusty carpet tiles. A birch stump in a red field. Her eyes blurred now, she had meant to tell Leo that she loved him. Now they'd turned the corner and she couldn't see him anymore. Richard took her elbow with his gentle grasp and led her toward the gate.

Two

At least there was the airplane food. Faye adored the trays they brought you. She always ordered vegetarian meals for them, as the quality tended to be better on Air Canada flights, at least. She loved all the little pots of this and packets of that to open, ingest, sip at and then leave a mess on the tray for somebody else to clean it up. Pure heaven.

Richard huffed and puffed over some containers and Faye liked to casually take the troublesome item out of his beleaguered paws and hey presto! She would open it by magic, and Richard would say, "Finally! Those things are the devil to deal with."

Faye loved feeling competent.

Once the tray was devastated, licked clean down to the plastic knife (why bother making the knives in plastic when you could easily stab someone to death with the metal fork?—more mass hysteria in this post-911 world), then the fun began with the movie channels, especially in business class. Faye eased back, sock slippers on, earphones in place so she wouldn't be party to Richard's performance of slipping in and out of sleep with snorts of consciousness and grunts of delirium, and surfed the channels until she'd figured out all twenty film narratives and decided on one that was suitably exciting yet not bone-chilling, hopefully amusing or slightly witty, to hold her attention for the first two hours, until she took her motion sickness pill and Morpheus flew her away.

Today, though, as they aimed for

Hawaii, flying over the hypocritical skies of North America, she daren't sleep, in case of a mutiny in the back of the plane, where she'd be the only alert passenger, with an eye on the credit card phone, ready to call out the Mounties. She kept her left knee steady against the phone all through dinner.

Despite her attempts at vigilance, within forty-five minutes Faye's head drooped onto Richard's shoulder and they slept curled together like small hibernators, while the plane hurtled over the patchwork prairies below.

By midday they landed in Vancouver for a three-hour stop, to change planes for the Vancouver-Honolulu leg. They headed for the Air Canada lounge, feet already swollen from the flight and a dizzy humming in Faye's left ear where she hadn't fully equalized yet. Richard found them space-age seats near the floor-to-ceiling windows overlooking fleets of planes lining up to get soaked under the steady, mind-destroying drizzle bearing down. Across the rest of Canada it would be snowing today, but oh no, not in Vancouver—here it always rained. Rained for nine months of the year. Faye sat down and rummaged in her handbag for her blood pressure pills.

"What would you like from the buffet?" Richard asked. She could hear his stomach rumble in happy anticipation of a snack.

"A banana, if they've got one that's not genetically-messed up. And a cup of tea." She was supposed to eat a banana daily, to help maintain potassium levels in conjunction with her blood pressure medicine.

Richard took a tray and she watched from across the room as he inspected muffins, sniffing one before choosing it, painstakingly producing hot water for a pot of tea. A member of the staff came over to help him. He was such a scarecrow of a man; people automatically assumed he was less robust than he appeared. Eventually he returned, leading the lounge attendant who carried their tray, colorful with treats. The promise of sugar.

It was the pinnacle of joy for people of their age, a cup of tea with a little something. Part of Faye rebelled against this slow semi-death of just eating and sitting like a lump in a corner, and part of her cried out to sit down and never stand up again.

She thanked the young man who placed the tray on the metallic table between their chairs. Richard was off again, scanning the newspaper rack, his nose crinkled like an accordion as he read lead stories through bifocals. Faye stirred the tea once, twice, leaving it to brew and slowly unpeeled and ate a small, perfectly pale yellow banana that had definitely been genetically-messed up. She could taste the difference between a lab banana and a Brazilian real McCoy.

Richard returned with his selected newspapers. She poured out the tea.

She watched him ingest a prune muffin by methodically turning down the crinkle paper 1/10th of a decimeter at a time. He baked an array of muffins himself and always loved to try out other variations.

"I do believe there's plain unsweetened yoghurt in this," he said, one mouthful in. Faye nodded. Richard's baking repertoire far exceeded her own. Being a former chemist, he called anything he'd made a product. He would concoct salads and proclaim, "There are six ingredients in this product," as he put it on the table, and children would groan, knowing that spring onion constituted one ingredient, the salad dressing another. He was good at dealing with lamb's fry, fish, chicken livers, anything with ventricles or veins, anything with a skeleton, anything that formerly twitched. Unfortunately certain kids had terrible luck in hitting every ventricle that he'd miss cutting out, causing them to retch and drag the pale bronchial veins out of their young disgusted mouths. Especially Ingrid. No wonder she turned vegan. Richard's porridge had staved off divorce for years. She would never leave his raisin porridge. They sat in their habitual almost-silence. Faye drank her tea and read her latest murder. Richard flicked through *The Vancouver Sun*.

"Look, Faye." He held up the Classifieds pages, a shaky finger pointed to a tiny ad: NANAIMO Ocean & Mtn view Level entry 2 storey 2550 FT 4br, 3ba, soaker, tub, alarm, huge lot RV prkg, $309K.

"What's the use of looking? We can't afford it."

They used to live in Nanaimo, in an architecturally designed three-bedroom house near lovely neighbors, in the wilds of Vancouver Island back then, but today, transformed into a cultivated suburban setting where prices had risen 800 percent since they'd owned their house. But when they lived here Faye couldn't stomach the wet soggy climate. They'd sold the house in Nanaimo in 1962 and immigrated by boat to the South Pacific. They made about $2,000 profit on the house, brilliant for those days.

"It's just interesting, is all."

"We should move to the Maritimes,

there's more sunshine out there. Better healthcare."

"I didn't say a thing."

Richard pretended all the time, but she knew him. He was the rolling stone. She had to work hard to keep crazy ideas knocked out of his mind, because once he'd decided on a course of action, neither hell nor high water would prevent him from stepping onto the plane, boat, or train.

It was a higher imperative that put him in motion. If he got some tomfool of an idea about moving back to Nanaimo in his head then he would worry it into shape, like a dog with a bone and once they had their tickets, he executed the maneuver without reflection, without a second thought. Strange for someone with zero military background.

Their flight was called: AC 93 to Honolulu. Richard dropped the newspaper.

"Come on," he huffed off his seat, his spindly arms pushing at the sides of the space-age seat to gain momentum.

"I don't want to go," Faye said. She remained seated and twisted her handbag strap around her fingers. She stared out the window at the heavy rain soaking the planes. These places she got caught in, they were terrifying and sickening. She wanted to turn back, go home, even if that silly rented house in Ontario didn't feel like home either, but it had her few things in it; that made it home.

"What do you mean?"

"This trip. We'll turn up at all these places and be designated a sofa bed and then we'll talk about nothing for X-amount of days before being ushered to the plane and then the tears will come out and I don't know why we're going to all this effort when undoubtedly we'll be told off for interfering."

"What interfering?" Richard's eyes watered. It was a reflex action to the heating, but Faye couldn't help feeling it was in part a response to her words.

"If I make *one* comment about anyone's children, house, job, life, husband, wife or miscellaneous then that's interfering. Never mind that I have to sit listening to all of them *wail* on about their useless X, Y and Z. But, no, I mustn't make a single comment or even nod my head. All of them. They're all the same. I'm not going. Why should I? What do they do for us?"

Richard seemed to know he couldn't sit down or the game would be up. He shuffled a bit, eyes wandering off to the departures screen. "Faye, the plane's boarding soon. Come on, it's all the way to

Gate 53."

"What if the plane crashes? Maybe I have a bad feeling about it."

"Come on now. Air Canada's only had that one problem when a plane caught on fire in 1983. And the loss of life wasn't that significant, I think it was only twenty people affected..."

"Affected? Don't you mean asphyxiated in a dark, smoke-choked plane?!"

"Alright, alright. They managed to land the thing."

"See? 1983 was the year Junie moved to Honolulu! That's an omen."

"They're a marvelous airline, really. And we've got the tickets, we have to go."

"If Junie starts complaining when we land, then I'll stay in my room the whole visit. No, what am I talking about, I'll stay on the couch the whole visit. You'll all have to sit around me. I won't budge. I'm warning you."

"Why warn me, dear? Talk to the offspring."

"They all hate me."

"What?" Richard's voice rose exponentially to the hyperbole of Faye's flat sentences. "That's baloney."

"Or, at least they blame me."

"Well, that's an entirely different issue," Richard said. He led them out the lounge, pushing Faye's colossal handbag in a trolley, ferreting out the boarding passes. He whistled Beethoven's *Eroica*. Faye was forced to walk quickly to keep up with him.

"It's not fair, why don't they ever get mad at you? You can't put a foot wrong. They assume I've psychologically traumatized them for either not putting starch on the bed sheets or for making us move all the time. They've got it all wrong. They've got *us* wrong."

"Now, now, not all of them. Besides, they only think that because your bark is the loudest. Law of nature. You're seen as the alpha-female."

"There's no such thing."

"Of course not. That's what's so ironic. Listen, we'll go visit everyone and we'll have a lovely time. If we have to sleep on a few couches, then so be it. Worse things have happened at sea. Besides, Junie said she has a small room for us. We can't let Junie down."

Faye rose from her seat. She never liked to let Junie down. Or any of the kids.

Junie had brought home a boyfriend once for a milk drinking session. She was six, they were still in the bowels of the North Island of New Zealand. It was 1963, and Faye was busy with the new baby, Will, whom they'd adopted in February. Junie walked in from school at precisely 3:08, followed by a rat-faced blond boy Faye had never seen before. Their one-level bungalow backed onto the school yard, so Junie always walked to and from school while Faye watched from the sky-blue painted kitchen. That afternoon, the scarce late sun sifted through – hazy with ozone that it still held, the Frigidaire hummed and rattled erratically, four-year-old Nadine was in the garden playing and toddler Matt was at the tail-end of his afternoon nap. The baby Will lay kicking on his quilt where Faye could keep an eye on him.

"Mum, can Simon stay?" Junie stood at the doorway with her little friend.

"What do you mean, stay? For the afternoon, sure."

"No, I mean, *stay*, like the baby

stayed."

"Drink some milk," Faye said, not wanting to make eye contact with the boy. He truly did look like a rodent. Buck-teeth, pointy chin, eyes scurrying around his skull, hair sticking up every which way. A stray. Junie carefully poured out milk into two tall glasses. She replaced the bottle in the Frigidaire and shut the metal door clasp with determination. She carried her and Simon's glasses out into the living room, on the kids' little table for tea parties.

"And where do you live, Simon?" Faye forced herself to ask. She cut up some cheddar cheese and apple into chunks and placed a small plateful on their table. Simon sniffed a morsel of cheese suspiciously.

"Over a road," he motioned absently. Great, she'd have to send Richard out with this kid later to locate his family. How could he not know where he lived? Mind you, Nadine will probably have the same trouble when she starts school next year, Faye sighed to herself.

Will drifted into an uneasy sleep, his fists curled into red balls. He slept fitfully and ate little. He had arrived into the world two months' premature, had weighed as much as a cantaloupe when born and lived in an incubator for his six weeks. Nadine and Matt filed into the living room and joined the others; Nadine curious about a newcomer, Matt wary and sleep-crusted.

Faye brought in more milk for her children.

Milk was everywhere in New Zealand. Cheese, butter, milk were cheap and stuffed with calcium. She turned the radio on for the children to listen to Howard Morrison singing *My Old Man's an All-Black* on Radio One and returned to finish the dishes and make a start on the potatoes for dinner.

It was a good half-hour later when the noises in the living room rose in pitch to strident fear. Faye put the potato peeler far back on the counter and looked to Will—a premature baby could have breathing difficulties—but he was fine. She rushed into the living room. Simon lay on his side, breathing hoarsely, his face was red, puffed up with white spots, his squinty eyes almost lost in the folds of bloated skin. Junie stood beside him, shrilling, "Mum! Mum!"

The younger two stared, slack mouthed, in shock, unmoving in their tiny chairs. Dribs of milk had spilled on the carpet. The cheese was all finished. Simon breathed as if through rags.

Faye scooped up the boy in her arms and turned to Junie, "You three. Go into the kitchen and sit by Will. I'm going next door. They have a phone."

She took off, cantering a funny gait over to the McKinleys at number 128, Simon swelling in her arms, his breath coming low and slow, he smelled sweet like turning milk. His arms flailed as Faye jogged, bouncing him regrettably.

"There, there, you'll be fine," she repeated, shielding his face from the sun.

Sally McKinley was in with her two boys. Faye beelined for her melamine black telephone and dialed before Sally could realize what the trouble was.

The hospital said they'd send round the doctor and the town ambulance.

"I'll wait at my place. My kids are on their own," Faye waved to Sally, racing out the door. Simon flailed in her arms. This kid was extremely allergic to dairy products. Something rarely seen in the sixties. There seemed nothing she could do except get him to a sink and induce vomiting.

Back inside, someone wailed. Matt, Faye realized, then he was joined by Will. In the kitchen, Junie had shoved Matt into his small chair too roughly, undoubtedly trying to make amends for poisoning her pal. Matt, still in shock, started crying. The domino effect knocked Will out of his sleep. Junie retaliated by sobbing herself. Only Nadine calmly played with the potato skins on the counter, lining them up for a talking-to, tottering on a small stool. Faye's peeler still lay beyond reach of the four-year old. She ignored the wailing trio crying and held Simon's face over the kitchen sink. Globs of Colby cheese swam out of his mouth, on a river of fetid milk. He choked up several chunks and a bowlful of liquid. His face was still puffed up like the

Michelin man, alternating white pockets with red streaks.

"Junie, honey? Where does Simon live?"

"I—I don't know!" the girl wailed.

"What's his last name?" Faye checked her watch. Doctor Harris should be there by now. Inglewood was a small town. Very small. Whose family did this child belong to?

"Jessup," Junie said, it sounded like a hiccup. Faye had swathed Simon in cold wet tea towels and wrapped his arms to his body like a dead Pharaoh, binding him in a towel just brought in off the line, when he started to scratch at his face with his short, blunt nails.

"Junie honey, can you go next door, to Mrs. McKinley's house and ask her to telephone Mr. and Mrs. Jessup? Tell Mrs. McKinley Simon's last name is Jessup. That's a good girl."

"Can I go too?" Matt's tears

stopped and dried in an instant.

"Me too?" Nadine chimed in. Her children didn't want to be around this sick child. This intruder who'd collapsed on their carpet. This strange boy who'd puffed up and stopped talking after his milk. Only Will wanted to stay, still grizzling from his blanket. Poor lamb needed picking up.

"Alright. All hold hands. Walk across the yard, not on the street."

The children left, with Matt hopping down the stairs, Junie in the middle, gripping onto hands like the Grim Reaper. Her mouth was set in a hard line and her left braid had come undone.

Faye finally heard the ambulance in the road. She held out a finger for Will to hold onto. Doctor Harris arrived just after the ambulance, they ran Simon over to the hospital and injected him with adrenaline to stop the anaphylaxis.

Richard walked in the door to find the four children dotted around the table eating fish cakes and mashed potato. Faye's kitchen held hints of disarray, but nothing was apparent to his eye.

"How was everyone's day?" he said, kissing the top of Faye's head and feeling the heat radiate off her skull.

"Junie brought a little friend over, but I think we won't be doing that again, right, kiddies?"

The trio nodded. Nadine jiggled her feet under the table. Matt picked off breadcrumbs from his fish cakes. Junie's eyes were wide with rue. Will gurgled from his bottle.

"It's a bother having friends over," Junie said.

Faye stretched from her ankles to her neck, stiff-limbed, like a cat.

Richard slept now, mouth whistling soft nothing words, his head crooked over his chest at an odd 45 degree angle that threatened to amputate his oxygen supply at any second. She stared out the tiny frosted rectangle, the light came into her eyes. It was pallid and thin, falling in trickles to hit the reinforced window. Unnatural, emaciated light. From this height it was unrecognizable, alien. There wasn't enough oxygen and it burned through the window to claw Faye's face. She closed the blind. Checked her international time/date clock. Another hour. She opened her book. Quite happy to be darting round the globe now, visiting her lovely children. Not sure why she'd gone on like that in the airport, perhaps the first hop-flight had made her dizzy, her ears weren't always the best on the short hops, leaving a disorientated muddle in her head. The stewardess noticed she was awake and offered her a juice, water or champagne. She selected the apple. Sipping slowly, the sugar fed her brain optimism, a sense of elation, visiting the kids! Going places! her brain stage-whispered. There would be moments of taking care of them. There would be moments of understanding her prodigy. There would be illumination and insight into their lives.

She took up her latest mystery to read, but soon put the murder on her lap. Even reading, thoughts intruded. She was hoping for something, that all the loose ties would be wrapped up. Some kids were loose ties. Some were wrapped up tight with their own natural strings of sense and reason and didn't need to be worried about. They were *fine*. Others were *troubled*. *So-so* kids oscillated in between, she couldn't seem to get a trace on them. *So-so, troubled, fine, so-so, troubled, fine, so-so.* Her seven worry beads lined up waiting to be pondered. That was her seven. And now the grandchildren were growing up, but she couldn't add them to her list. Sienna, the oldest grandchild, Nadine's, was the only one she really had to take care of. She'd practically raised that child when Nadine was off on her flights of fancy to Italy for art school. That kid had deserved more stability. It wasn't easy on Sienna.

She took out the plane tickets to hold them in her hands. Every page another child. How had they been spread so far? Junie, the oldest, a self-proclaimed worrier living a hippie life in Honolulu, how had she forgotten that stop? Will holding the fort in Auckland waiting for some big homecoming, Sienna was there too, not technically her baby but close enough, Sienna who didn't have a job, who slept until 11.11 everyday, who had her father and her mother in her which was a terrible mix at times. Then the big reason for the trip, the excuse all the rest hung off, seeing Ingrid in Sydney hopefully in time to help with her new baby, although helping Ingrid had always been a tug-of-war. Leave the Southern Hemisphere and scoot up to Dubai, to find Skye, who worked doing some job she never talked about, they hadn't seen her for three years now. And London, her favored city that thrilled and scared her, to see Matt— stable as chips Matt. The last page took them back full circle to Montreal, to Leo and Nadine. What could she do for Nadine at the end of this all? She'd tried. Nadine distrusted her immensely. There were no topics left between them that Nadine didn't flare up about, accusing her, accusing her of interfering.

The Ventures daughters had something about interference. Mainly they craved attention and then repudiated it as soon as they had Faye's full consideration.

Faye caressed the thick tickets. They would be picked up at every airport, well, except Sydney, Australia as Ingrid *couldn't*. They would stay and visit and she would learn things she hadn't known, or at least listen for the words behind the words, especially from Skye who she suspected was involved in something odd; and Matt who seemed too good to be true, in her murder novels that always meant something being kept secret, something she wouldn't want to think too much about. Even Junie, there was something hidden and worrying about her new life. Will was impossible to know. He had put up a wall since, since a time Faye couldn't remember. And Sienna might be taking drugs and probably drank alcohol.

Faye's hand had pins and needles. She put the tickets back in their sleeve, back in the outer zippable pocket so they wouldn't be lost. She felt torn apart, traveling away from her base into the wilds. Happy nowhere, if she admitted it to herself. She turned to Richard. He'd talk the troubled ones down off their ledges. He'd smooth things over with the ones who now repudiated their mother. He'd sort some of them out. Perhaps. One could hope. Richard, who'd taken a wooden spoon to the kids maybe on one occasion in their lives. The man who represented the opposite of discipline. He had rigor, but fostered a devil-may-care lark-about-the-world-as-you-like shiftiness. Probably distilled down from his Viking and Huguenot ancestry.

Faye was, in truth, scared.

Three

They landed in Honolulu and found the arrivals hall. The room had low ceilings, but fans circulated chilled air throughout. Fake leis were dolled out by the Hawaiian Tourist Board by women past their prime wearing traditional costumes that displayed fattened hips not round from dancing that was for sure. The public relations gimmick felt like boat trips from the eighties. What a cheesy place. The Polynesian islands used to promise a natural warmth, connectedness, sense of earthy goodness... but Hawaii had been tainted and turned into a gaudy souvenir shop by America long ago. Most of Honolulu lived in air-con. The beaches were overpopulated. They had to truck in the sand. The volcanoes had given up the ghost. Faye couldn't understand why Junie lived here. That had never made a jot of sense.

Junie burst upon them.

"Mum, Dad."

"So there you are," Richard said, he leaned in to kiss Junie's cheek. Her eyes shined with emotion. Faye hugged her, gripping the thin shoulders and gave her a kiss on the other cheek that Richard missed.

"Have you got something in your lens?" Faye asked, assuming that the air-conditioning blew dust in Junie's contact lenses.

"No! I'm just happy you're here." She took their trolley and pointed to the automatic doors. There were questions about the flight that Richard handled. Faye was struck how her child's voice had a certain needling quality to it that she didn't like particularly. Junie had a smooth, low, slightly British, semi-Canadian accent that held great appeal. It was a stellar accent that matched her courageous personality. But when Junie gained adulthood and married Yann, her voice took on a supplicating tone. The timbre of it set Faye's teeth on edge. Yann must've developed it in her. Neither she nor Richard had a tone like that. And they'd lived through the Great Depression, the war years, the fifties conservatism in Canada that had driven Faye mad with desperation. But no, they didn't have that tone. It belonged to Junie and she'd cultivated it. That was environment versus nature.

She wheeled them through the doors and the heat knocked into Faye as if it were a rude passerby pushing against her whole body in an instant. The palms swayed drunken hellos. The car park shimmered like a mirage of mirrors, bright fenders, metallic paint colors. Junie found her car, an old station wagon, flecked a palomino color. Or flecked with mud. It lay low to the tarmac and had Macbeth-red leather seats that had cracked in several places. She placed their hand luggage in the boot carefully.

"I can't believe they lost your luggage. What a pain we'll have to come back tomorrow," Junie lamented.

Faye had failed to mention that she'd checked them plus luggage all the way to Auckland.

"Yes, lousy airline, I think it's to do with some baggage handling strike," Faye fibbed. White lies padded out her relationship with certain kids, she found. Most of the kids, in fact.

She surveyed the trunk of the car. It was lined with junk to its farthest reaches. Unidentifiable junk. Bits of paper, empty wrappers, sand galore, an old netball, cracked goggles without the strap, the lenses cracked and strapped to each other, lost and unloved. Their hand luggage, although nothing fancy, was in danger of being scuffed and dirtied among the rubble. Faye sighed. Nothing to say about that.

The inside of the car was little better. Junie's girls had strewn the floor in the back with the same flotsam. Torn reading books, a crushed Coca-cola bottle with a sickly residue coating its side, broken toys lying next to scattered raisins and potato chips. How did they get the car in such a state? Richard stretched his legs over similar detritus in the front passenger seat. Junie fastened her seatbelt with an eager smile.

"How about a tour of the new café development at the waterfront before we go up to the house?"

Faye wanted to say she was too tired. Richard soothed an affirmative response. Damn it all. Couldn't they relax first and be dragged around the island later? The air in the car was stifling. The smell of crushed frangipani flowers mingled with sweaty forgotten socks. It was a horrible scent of festering dirty things. Left to rot.

"You'll have to roll down the windows, Mum. The air-con is broken."

As soon as the windows were opened, the wind snatched all words from the front quarter and Faye could hear nothing. She swallowed hard. Her ears still hadn't fully balanced. She wondered if she might be sick, or faint. She tried swallowing again. The sickly feeling wasn't from flying. The crew were professionals back there, in that lovely cool clean plane they'd left. It was being trapped in this cesspit with the wind and Junie taking the curves too fast. Everyone drove too fast and it merely revved up Faye's imagination. The car sliced around a winding back road, cicadas screeched in the scrubby bush, replanted palms pocked here and there, then a sea vista, the Pacific heavy with power, waves storing up their fury to smash into the sand, it was sad in a way—the water gathering itself up into a frenzy like that, flecking at the mouth, a curvature of self-expression deepening and rising, the peak a brand new mountain for the moment—and then there was nowhere else to go and it crashed into the shoreline, a Kamikaze pilot, a spent life, a briefly amazing thing reduced to froth. Faye saw it all as countless near spins out of control—the car narrowly missing potholes that would spin them upside down, and the sea view as a heavy reminder of a tsunami hitting the coast one day and sweeping all those condos and bars and cafes into oblivion.

The vista disappeared in a dark green blur. They were descending a hill now and Faye could feel her daughter's foot pumping the brake pedal, why pump it? For God's sake just *brake*, Faye's head filled with frantic thoughts, pumping the pedal means maybe it's not working properly. Don't tell me your banged up wreck of a car doesn't have good brakes. O, and this hill was a Himalaya. She noticed Richard's right hand had sneaked up and now gripped onto the coat rail, the veins were stark, raised blue protruding from his sinewy hand.

"Can't you slow down, honey?" Faye called. She wasn't even sure they could hear her. "Honey? Kiddo?

Slow down."

Richard made some observation about the flora or the industry of bees. Junie was relaxed, slouching even, her foot still pumped the brake, in third gear but rolling fast, corners swelled up before the nose of the car and were somehow turned, the road signs flashed by advising 25, 20, even 15 mph.

Faye's two hands gripped the front seats, she reached for Richard's shoulder, shouting, "Junie, slow down!"

Her child turned to look at her, not even looking at the road, "Why, Mum? It's perfectly fine. I'm not going fast."

Richard peered backwards, his face squinted through his spectacles, "Are you uncomfortable back there? Do you want to sit up in the front?"

"No! For Godssake, Ingridskyenadinejunie, slow right

down. Please."

Faye often let out a stream of children's names before alighting on the appropriate one. She did it with all the kids. The boys got a barrage that included her own father's name and Richard's, before their own. Her brain just couldn't think what she'd named any one of them sometimes.

Junie slowed to a crawl. The wind stilled outside. A honking came from behind from idiot irritated drivers.

"Let them pass us," Faye urged.

"Mum, I can't, there's nowhere to pull over."

But the resourceful girl found a driveway to duck into so the honkers' cars could whir past.

"Do you still want to go see the development? Because we could go home right now, if you want." Junie's voice had a grumpy ring to it. A threatening edge that warned they would go home if behavior wasn't modified right then and there. Faye's eyes wandered the backseat area, her lips lifted into a hint of a pout; she had never voiced enthusiasm for seeing the development anyway. Home, she just wanted to go home. Her home. Too far. Okay then, any home.

"Yes, let's go home. We've been flying for fifteen hours. We had to sit in Vancouver for three hours. We can go see the development tomorrow."

"Well," Junie shoved the car into reverse and backed out onto the road superfast to turn around, "I picked up the girls yesterday so we'll have them for half of this week, but then they go back to their father's on Wednesday, so I just wanted to show it to you today, before we get home because then we'll be too busy with things with them, they want to show you their school and their favorite beach and their favorite café towards the north side and that's miles from Waikiki, so I just wanted to show it to you today, but *if* you're tired," Junie said, as if Faye was putting it on— faking some show of tiredness after earlier not saying that she was tired, as if it was a sudden and perhaps pretended fit of tiredness to thwart Junie's plans—"*if you're tired*, then we should go home. I just have to pick up a few things from the store."

That tone had taken up residence in her voice again. Faye's teeth crushed into each other. A shiver ran over her body. It may have been a reaction to the sudden tropical heat after Ontario's steady crisp decline into minus figures, but it was more likely revulsion at Junie's tone. Faye stared out the window at the blurring houses set back from the road behind gates and she fought off tears. They rose up like a hot bubbling cauldron inside her, making her face steam and her breath come in quick pants, like a dog's. Her child made her fight for breath like a dog when she upset her like this. She fought off the tears, knowing that if one slipped then that would be the end of the charade and the visit would be awful, and knowing that if one didn't slip she would break into pieces in the hot backseat of this befouled car. She felt a tiny trickle out the corner of her right eye. It wound its way into her ear. She squeezed her eyes shut tight. That was all that she was allowed.

They soon pulled into a mall's parking area and Junie hopped out of the car, keys in hand, turning back to them, smiling again.

"Aren't you going to come in? It's cool inside. I just have to pick up a few things."

"Approximately long are you going to be?" Richard asked.

"Not long. Two minutes."

Faye knew this would have to be a blatant lie. But she couldn't move. She'd rather lie in the back, panting like a dog and die there than move around the supermarket while a cart grew full and the few things prompted more things and the more things reminded Junie of other things. She hated Hawaii.

"I'll stay in the car."

"Me too," said Richard.

Junie softened; she sat back down in the driver's seat. She patted her father's arm—hopefully not with any force since the man bruised at the drop of a hat these days, large terrifying bruises like a blood vessel had exploded under the skin. Bruises the color of these Macbeth-red seats. Junie beamed at them both. A new fancy had taken her mind.

"It's okay, we can go home now, I'll get Sean to go to the store. You're both exhausted, aren't you? It's too hot here."

"That would be lovely, honey," Faye said. "If you don't mind."

She often had to call her kids honey; it was part of that problem with not remembering their names. And if sometimes she called them honey through gritted teeth, then that was just part of being a parent.

Junie was pleased with herself. She started up the car. Richard's hand drooped from the coat rail and he allowed his head to slump forward for a few moments then jerk upright again. He was having a 'micro-nap.' Faye wanted to join him. A breeze found its way inside the car finally as Junie steered them on to yet another road and Faye hoped that her house was around the next corner.

Five

They arrived at a bungalow set on a jungled quarter-acre patch. This was the New House that Junie had bought with the New Boyfriend, Sean. Faye and Richard hadn't seen this kid for a year and a half and in that time she'd left Yann in their architect-designed mansion to this decidedly different, almost child's version of a house. It immediately reminded Faye of their house in Rotorua, where Leo almost drowned in the swimming pool, it was a low-to-the-ground house almost like a dog crouching at your heels.

Junie had moved from Sing Sing (as they called her home with Yann because she felt imprisoned there) and this was her new beginning at the age of forty-three, with her two girls and the new boyfriend. Faye and Richard had heard his voice on the phone, for intermittent commercial-length intervals between long monologues from Junie about all the horrors of a modern divorce when you lived in the States and your ex-husband plays hardball and manipulates the girls, fought for shared custody, spied on you, lied about you, got the neighbors to "testify." Faye agreed it hadn't been easy. But then, divorce was a thousand times easier today than a certain time. She'd almost said on the phone, I told you so, I never felt comfortable around Yann. You had second doubts before you got married. You should never have gone through with it. But, that would be unnecessary and cruel. She was on Junie's side, of course. And hindsight was always 20/20.

"Here we are," Junie carefully

turned off the car. She sat for a moment. She seemed nervous to show them her new life. For them to meet Sean, or see how few of her knick knacks she'd salvaged from Sing Sing, to place here, in the Little Shack? Or was she going to have one of her heart-to-hearts here, in the car, about some new horror Yann was inflicting on them, or some other never-seen-before disaster that plagued her?

"Nina is on Ritalin—because of the custody battle," she said stiffly and got out of the car.

Richard turned to Faye, "Do you think it's possible I left my second pair of glasses on the bedroom windowsill?"

"I would say it's very possible. Even probable," Faye nodded.

"Methylphenidate is readily-prescribed cure these days," Richard mused.

She loved Richard when his science made sense of family.

A dog bounded for them. Junie had always had a black Lab. When she was a baby, they'd had one and when the dog died fourteen years later, Junie went through a hiatus for ten years until she and Yann got another black Lab when they were married. When that one died, a short life of six years, she got another. And another when Lab III was run over. This was perhaps black Lab mark five. They were all named Abby.

This Abby rippled with muscle as she bounded. She was fully grown with a glossy coat, probably related to egg yolk shampoos or some such foolery. Faye edged back against the car, worried that Abby would crush her, or bruise Richard. The dog's forelegs heaved with a solid power to bruise.

"Abby! C'mon, baby! C'mon, baby!"

Junie was bent lifting bags from the trunk. The call came from the porch, where little Nina slapped her thighs in her attempt to draw Abby away from her grandparents. Little Nina was now seven and looked like a street hooker. The child had painted herself with make-up. Clown's blush and electric mauve lipstick. Her eyes were further swamped by unsuitable silver glitter that caked her lids. The hair was the same. Infinitely long, wavy and a dull red. Nobody could convince Nina to ever cut it. She was keen on some world record for hair length. Today, in the perpetual humidity, it was half down, hiding her bottom and straggling to the back folds of her knees, and half up in one Princess-Leia pretzel on the top of her head. It sparkled with gold glitter that had been liberally doused over it. There was so much hair that it made her look one foot tall. Faye frowned at Abby, who slowed to a graceful walk and gently sniffed at Faye's hand, taking one dainty lick. Then the dog circled to Richard and nuzzled near his crotch adoringly. Faye smiled a tight, embarrassed line of greeting.

"Well, hello Nina!" she used her sing-song voice reserved for unknown situations with relatives. Nina lumbered down the brief stairs and hugged Faye, crushing her.

"Gramma!"

The child lunged for Richard next, who instinctively sidestepped to put Abby between them, "Grampa!"

"Easy there, Nina. I bruise like an overripe peach."

Humor stopped Nina. "Really? Lemme see!"

Richard offered his forearm which he'd recently knocked slightly getting out of their shub. It was deep scarlet under the thin skin.

"Ewwwww!" Nina pretended to gag, "Mom, Grandpa's arm is bleeding internally!"

"Never mind," Junie said, and Faye was reminded of herself. How many times had she said those words to her own children?

Their small bags now lay in the dust of the driveway. The adults parceled them out among each other and Nina led the way, the bloody mess of her grandfather's arm now long forgotten in her delight of playing Real Estate Tour Guide to show them the house. Abby trotted off, with slighted feelings. As Faye would too, if she were a black Lab, fifth in line to a dream dog.

They were shown the front room, or the Playroom. It had wooden floorboards painted over in white, blue accents on the sofa, the bookshelf stuffed with an eclectic wash of spine sizes including several copies of Junie's bestselling series. The television took up the other half of the room. There was no toy in sight.

"What do you play in here?" Richard asked.

"This is where I host my YouTube channel: *Disney by Nina*," Nina smiled. It was a game, Faye assumed. They were led into the "Lounge/Diner". Nina sounded like a Hollywood estate agent in stilettos tottering around an open home with a cigarette dangling from rouged lips.

"Note the projector for home movies, this sofa is the most comfortable, but Abby and I usually take that one. The dining table seats six. That's how many we are with you two: six. So that's the maximum for the table. I am the only one who plays the piano over there. It was Sean's mother's—but she gave it to me. Except Mommy plays sometimes to show me things. The French windows lead onto the Outside Patio where we have a real water fountain and the fish pond, but we lost two of the carp last week. Sean said it was the algae. Now here, we go through to the Kitchen. The Powder Room is to the left."

Richard aborted the tour and disappeared without comment for bodily relief. Nina seemed not to notice.

The kitchen was all accented in blue as well. White and blue. Her daughter had always wanted to live in Greece. On Santorini or Crete specifically. She had been to Greece once, with Yann, when they'd tossed a coin in Gare du Lyon to decide between Barcelona and then down to Morocco—or Nina and the ferry over to Greece. Tails had won. But they'd gotten so seasick on the ferry that Junie had to be hospitalized in Patras and flown back to Heathrow. They never made it to the islands. But she had seen a lot of magazines.

"We grow our own organic chili, organic chives, organic basil, organic parsley, would you like some now?" She ripped a fistful of chives and chomped on them with determination.

"Not right now, Nina, Gramma and Grampa are tired."

Richard rejoined the group and opened random kitchen cupboards. Junie pulled a face. Richard halted his inspection. No doubt he was searching for supplies of rolled oats and wheat germ for the morning porridge.

Nina pirouetted down the hallway, picking up a pink fairy wand on the way. It was Barbie pink and when the girl flicked on a switch and swung the object violently, it trilled a grating melody that Nina repeated,

"Brrrrrrrrrrrrrrrrrring!!!!!"

"I'm taking modern dance. So's Sophie. Here we have Sophie's room. Without Ensuite..."

The room was a muted violet with a brown bedspread over a double bed. It was more barren than Faye imagined a teenager's room to be. The windows were shuttered and a smell of socks and one of those perfumes for girls hung around the edges of the room.

"Sophie's out with Sean, they'll be back very soon! Next is Mom and Sean's room, with Ensuite. Note the stained glass windows and the fourteen-inch television, which pivots. The spa bath is so wonderful." Nina kicked strewn clothes off the laundry hamper with her trilling wand, dispensing wishes on every bathroom item. She spun around, dizzy with happiness.

"This is my favorite room in the

house," she sighed.

Again, the blue and white motif dominated. Hanging plants gave a subtropical feel and blue mosaic tiles recalled Sing-Sing's tiled Master Bathroom.

"Aren't these tiles exactly like the ones...?" Faye asked Richard.

"Yes," Nina breathed, "like back at home. Yes. Mommy stole them." She looked thrilled beyond all reason as she circled around the spa bath, her fingers caressing.

"Then there's my room. This way." Nina's room backed onto Junie's and was a riot of reds, deep purples and highlighted with yellow of all things. Some crazed creature had recently played dress-ups in here and the gray carpet sparkled with glitter that Faye had seen in the girl's hair. Real make-up sat on the dressing table. Real powder puff and real lipstick. Real mascara. All better quality than

Faye herself possessed.

"This is my room. Do you like it?"

Faye noted another television lurked in a corner. So far Sophie's room was the only one without one. That and the kitchen.

"Did you decorate yourself?" Richard asked.

"Yes. I picked out everything. Except the carpet," she kicked at the dark gray. "That was already here and Mommy said we couldn't rip it out. I don't have an Ensuite," Nina said woefully.

"Well," Faye said, "We'd better go find your mom."

"You can put your things in Sophie's room. *She's* giving you her room," Nina said with a sudden harsh ring in her voice.

"O, isn't that nice?" Faye automatically reached for her calm voice.

Nina seemed eased and led them,

skipping, back to the kitchen. Faye realized that the girl had been embarrassed that she hadn't given up her room. Made to feel embarrassed. Or guilty, perhaps. Nina helped take their bags into Sophie's room. Faye went into the kitchen. Junie was on a cordless telephone, rattling off a list of grocery items while she emptied the dishwasher.

"No, no. Not the plain type. Vanilla flavored. Yes. Yes. Okay. I love you. Bye."

Faye had never heard her daughter say those words to a man. She said them all the time at the tail-end of phone conversations with her and Richard, but Faye usually mumbled some response like, "You too, take good care, honey." To say take good care always seemed more important than to actually say *I-love-you*. What if there was an accident? It was vital to say, Take Good Care. That was what mattered most. To take care. Be well. Be in one piece.

Junie started to tell Faye something, but stopped herself.

"Do you want a cup of tea?"

Finally. "Yes, please."

"We can all sit down outside, I'll make afternoon tea. Where's Dad?"

"Oh, he's probably looking for his second glasses," Faye's hands were at a loss, they felt as if they should be doing something, being in a kitchen. They started opening cupboards randomly.

"Don't worry, I've got everything," Junie said, her hands expertly unearthed mugs, teaspoons, a small blue and white plate.

Richard entered holding his transistor radio; he'd taken his shirt off and stood in a singlet that had seen a dozen summers. The thin cotton clung to its original form by only some miracle. His arms still held reasonable muscle tone. He wasn't an overweight man, but his paunch was noticeable. Faye told him all the time to try sit-ups. But there he was with his intestines threatening to spill over his belt.

"Richard, for God's sake, put some clothes on."

"I just need about four D-size batteries, Junie, if you have them. I can't find the AC outlet in the room. Just if you have four handy."

"The plug's beside the bed, on the right hand side," Junie said.

"Alright then, I'll make a second attempt to source it," he huffed and wandered off.

"Put your clothes back, you damn fool," Faye called after him. "You can't meet Sean in that state!"

"Mum, please don't swear, Nina will hear it," Junie said quietly.

"Swear? Damn isn't a swear word,

is it?"

Her daughter had tea things ready on a wooden tray, "Nina! Come and have some tea with the grown-ups," she called. "Of course it's a swear word."

"But he *is* a damn fool. Think of it as a pet name."

Junie's forehead crept into a frown again, "It's not nice to talk to Dad like that."

Faye felt a scream rise up in her. Not that she would scream. But it was there. She forced a gay smile onto her face, "Sure, honey, alright. I'll call him a dear fool if you like." She gestured for her daughter to walk first so she could follow. They sat near the water fountain. Nina joined them, slouching on the two-seater wicker sofa. Richard came out, still in his singlet.

"Oh, Ginger Snaps. My favorite."

"I know," Junie smiled.

He selected two and turned away, "I'm going to listen to my radio program while I can still pick it up and probably have a short nap. Wake me when the others arrive home."

Faye said nothing. Let Junie deal with him. This was a holiday, right? Chance for the kids to see their father?

"He's in such remarkable shape, isn't he? For eighty-five, I mean?"

"Well, he doesn't like to complain." No use mentioning the beta blockers his doctor had put him on just to keep his heart beating, or else it would just forget to beat most likely. Or that prostrate concern. That seemed to be settled anyway. Or the cataract operation that nearly went sour and cost him his sight. Or his general vagueness that came and went in waves of soundless frequency that Faye was actually frightened of. She smiled and nodded.

"Sure, kiddo. Strong as an ox. Don't you worry about your father."

"No, I mean he really is in good shape, I mean compared to Grampa Jimmy when he came to stay with us before he died. He was only, what, seventy?"

"Seventy-two. But he smoked." Richard's father used to sneak out for cigarettes and come in ruffling the kids' hair with the smell on his hands. Then cough for twenty minutes. Emphysema.

"But it wasn't just that," Junie said, "His stomach wasn't good."

"That was only when he went to live on Waiheke Island with those hippies and they feed him only wholemeal foods. It ended up perforating his stomach. That's what killed him in the end."

"I remember when we went up to see him in the hospital. And he died the next day. But you were about to give birth to Skye and didn't go. You didn't see how sad Dad was. He couldn't speak. I couldn't either. I cried all the way home."

"You? Why did you cry? You'd only met him a few times."

"Because when he came to live with us, I didn't want anymore people in the house. There was already four kids and Ingrid was almost two and you were about to have another baby. I used to put salt in his tea instead of sugar. And hide his things."

Junie poured milk into the cups. Neither of them touched the ginger snaps. Nina had already snaffled up four or so.

"Well, you were only fifteen. It wasn't your fault." Faye wondered if the sugar bowl was laced with salt. Was this a warning that Sophie and Nina could be expected to trip up and harass Richard? What was Junie getting at? She waited to listen between the words for the point to all this.

"That's true, Mom. It was your fault. You didn't want Grampa Jimmy living with us. I heard you complain about him all the time. You hated his smoking around the kids. Said it was all his second wife's fault he'd had to leave Canada. Told Dad to stick up for him and get his house back or he and Uncle Eddie would be left with nothing. Which they were. It was your negativity that I picked up on. I was acting out how you actually felt. And then I felt bad when he died. And you got everyone involved with that drama of adopting babies when Skye was born. And we all forgot about Grampa."

"What's all that got to do with Richard's state?"

"Well, Mum, I just wonder what are you and Dad going to do when you get too old to take care of yourselves? I just need to know, to make my own plans. I assume you'll want to stay with the nearest capable child..."

"O brother," Faye waved her arms at a mosquito she glimpsed in the periphery. She swelled up like a balloon with one bite. "Don't you worry about that. We'll be fine. It's all taken care of."

It wasn't, but she refused to be bullied into this conversation. How dare Junie pretend that she'd tormented Richard's father? And then to insinuate that they were going to dump themselves on the nearest child and just rot in some bedroom and be tortured by their grandchildren. 'Nearest capable child' meaning her. Nobody would count Nadine. And Leo was the youngest. Why bring all this up when she hadn't even finished her first cup of tea?

"Do you have any mosquito stuff? I'm going to get eaten alive."

Junie nodded, "Nina, can you get the cream from my Ensuite? Go on, now."

Nina had listened avidly to every word between the adults. She didn't want to miss the show. She slid off the sofa and stomped off into the house. Junie's kids were so heavy-footed; they'd gotten that from Richard's side too. Couldn't lift their legs properly to gently land on the floor. It was always a herd of elephants.

"Don't you think you shouldn't let her eat all those biscuits? It's pure sugar, you know. And butter."

"I only bought them for Dad. Normally we never have any cookies in the house," Junie retorted.

"Well, what is the kid eating to get in that shape? Does she do any exercise?"

Nina tromped through the French doors again, "Here, Gramma," she tossed the lotion in Faye's lap.

She inspected the bottle for signs of tampering. She suddenly didn't trust Nina. Was she going to sabotage Faye's things and switch products on her because of overhearing her mother's fears of Faye moving in one day and being a burden on them? She got the impression that Junie wouldn't mind Richard moving in, but her mother would be, just, too much. She slowly rubbed some of the oily substance on her ankles, her wrists, her calves. She hoped the creatures wouldn't bite her through her slacks.

"Do you want me to rub some on your neck, Gramma?" Nina asked.

"No, no. It's fine," Faye grimaced, "Thanks, Nina."

Junie sat without any emotion now,

staring mainly into her cup. It was half full. But Faye knew her daughter would think of it as half empty.

Sounds erupted from the driveway. Abby barked and a car door slammed. Junie's head jerked up, "They're home."

Faye went into Sophie's room to wake Richard. He lay on his back, breathing loudly, a see-saw of life still in him. She didn't want to wake him. The room was now permeated with Richard's trademark scent of Quik-Eze digestion tablets, chalky pale circles that dissolved on your tongue and a whiff of something Old Spice-like that he passed off as after-shave.

"Richard. They're here."

He woke instantly, "Where?" he asked.

"Out there. You'd better get dressed now. We don't want to scare Sean."

He obediently swung out of bed

and dragged on his pants and shirt. His awful bruises were on display. He sighed like a little boy.

"Richard? Was I really nasty about your father coming to stay with us in Rotorua? Did I force him to leave and go live on Waiheke and eat all that wholemeal food until it destroyed him?"

Six

"What's all this about? You were nothing of the sort. We just had too many in the house. And you were about to have Skye. It was too much for us. He wanted to go to Waiheke. He was painting again there. It was his last happy time." Richard sat back down on the bed. He patted Faye's hand, "You may have been a little sarcastic, but that's perfectly normal. I was about your mother."

"Yes, well. Junie seems to have some rather warped recollection of the whole thing."

"People generally do. That was thirty years ago. I wouldn't let it bother you."

"There's something odd going on with Junie. She's aggressive."

"She's been through some changes. Started over. I'd say it's a good thing compared to when she was agreeing with Yann twenty-four hours a day. Come along. Are there any of those Ginger Snaps left or did Nina ingest them all?"

They opened the door and Sophie stood there, patiently waiting. Faye hoped they'd spoken quietly enough.

"Hello Gramma. Hi Grampa." She hugged them both, squeezing without reasonable restraint for their age. She stepped back. Dear Sophie, Faye thought, the beautiful girl. She had put on weight, but there were still the flashing brown eyes, the angelic smile, and the lustrous brown wavy hair. She had more of Yann's looks. She ran off and dragged Abby over to them.

"Look, it's Abby. You remember Abby?"

Sophie hugged the dog hard. Abby

whistled a sigh and lay flat on the ground to wriggle out of the strong loving embrace. Sophie smiled, a disarming lopsided smile that reminded Faye of fifties movie stars, of Lauren Bacall crossed with Audrey Hepburn. Her thick dark lashes drooped prettily, "You want to meet Sean? He's over there."

She led them to the Lounge/Diner where Sean stood, waiting with a nervous stance.

"Well, glad to meet you, Sean. At last," Richard shook his hands, laughing then almost choking with his gruff emotion. He really was a sentimental sop. Any new acquaintance was greeted with tears of joy.

"Hello, Sean. It's great to finally meet you." Faye shook his hand also. Sean leaned in and gave her three kisses, one cheek, the other, and then the first one again. Faye felt dizzy again turning her head to keep up. Was there something wrong with her ears after that flight? She pushed at the flesh around her eardrum. Swallowed hard again.

"Let's all sit outside for an aperitif," Sean announced.

Well, he was already several points ahead on Yann. He hadn't sulked upon introduction, had displayed warmth and a generosity of spirit and a plain sanity that Yann hadn't really displayed even at first meeting. And he so casually invited them all to sit outside and perhaps she could have half a shandy or a tiny glass of port, and it seemed to be without fuss, drama or more sulking. It was as if he were genuinely happy to meet them. Junie was noticeably more relaxed with him in the room. The girls ran off into the Playroom. Junie called after them, "Come on, girls, we're going outside for an aperitif."

"That's okay," Sean said, "let them play. We'll all have conversation at dinner."

Conversation at dinner, that wasn't Yann's bag at all. More like stiff silent recriminations flying like daggers between family members, bar Richard, who had always been immune to any guilt complex and emphasized everyone's good qualities, like a prowess with gardening. Scientific mutual admiration, she supposed. Yann had studied his Masters in Genetics.

Faye shut her eyes. She didn't want to think about all that. She concentrated on Sean, who poured out little glasses of muscadet and passed around sun-dried tomato dip with organic wheat-free breadsticks. The olives were 'kalamata' whatever that meant. He was clearly devoted to Junie, his smile, although a thin line across his face, was its most endearing when turned in her direction. He wasn't too much of anything—not tall, not short, not thin nor rotund, he had three earrings and a strange necklace of aqua shells around his neck—possibly made by Junie, best not to comment on that— and wore purplish clothes with leather thongs. A definite Hippie, but sweet as sugar. No salt in him.

She sat back, pleased for a change. She felt lighter being around Sean. He joked, told stories, laughed like a horse, but that was somehow pleasant, too. And Junie didn't talk with that tone. She felt like they might have a lovely visit here.

Seven

Faye had a shoddy sleep the first night in Junie's bungalow. She and Richard loped off, exhausted, at eleven. The others all stayed up, watching a movie on the projector. Faye woke at half past midnight, hearing them all go to bed. Then at three, for the toilet, then at four from a bad dream of burglars breaking into the bungalow and shooting everyone. Then at five, she thought she heard a noise. And at five-thirty, she was fully awake.

Richard had similar troubles. At five-thirty he said he was going to go make some porridge and shuffled off in a bathrobe and old pajamas borrowed from Junie until their bags turned up. He wore Sophie's slippers that she'd insisted he use. The fifth Abby was heard whining in the kitchen. Faye heard Richard soothe the animal and they went out for a brief walk. Faye lay in bed, too tired to get up. Mulling things over. Junie was angry about something. Almost petulant and showing off like a child. But she was never like that as a child. She was sociable, caring, too caring. She heard the dog and Richard shut the kitchen door.

The dog's bark reminded Faye of the first Abby, who had been Junie's guardian angel in black fur. Dramatic things had happened with a strange ease to Junie.

She thought of that rotten kid Evan Williams. He was about seven or eight when Junie was five. Only child, a bit spoiled. Faye was baby sitting him while his parents and Richard went to a Unitarian church meeting.

She thought it was safe to let them play down in the basement, although Evan had already tried to scare Junie with a viewfinder showing Snow White and the wicked witch with the apple. That had put her daughter off any red fruit for a few years.

Evan emerged from downstairs.

"Where's Junie?" Faye asked him.

"Oh, she's still playing." The boy slunk out the door and out into the yard. There were no further noises. The house was utterly silent. Then Abby, the first Abby, began to bark. She followed the noise down to the basement and there stood a large trunk. Abby barked at it, running in circles. Pounding and screaming came out of it. The top was locked. Faye pulled at it with her fingers, clawed at it, but couldn't get it open.

She ran upstairs and outside, calling, "Can somebody come and help me? Please come and help?"

Two neighbors' husbands poked their heads out of doors. Faye was frantic. They ran over, downstairs and ripped open the trunk.

Junie was screaming in fear. She was fine though. She repeated senseless words about the witch being after her. The Snow White witch. She choked on her words. Her face streamed red with hot tears. Her long braids were tangled.

Faye looked inside the trunk. It was three-quarters full of her old clothes from her early twenties. Dating back to 1951 after the War. When she'd moved to England, then Germany. Her child had been surrounded by colorful corsets and boned brassieres and pastel petticoats from another era in Faye's life. Junie lay on it all like a sacrificial lamb, a still born calf and her eyes had screamed along with her mouth. But, she was fine. No damage done. Faye went back down into the basement later when the kids were in bed and refolded her things that had been mussed and wrinkled.

Richard took the kids out on their sailboat when they lived in Rotorua. The *Tamahere* was a 35-foot ketch, beautiful, they'd refitted her themselves. The first time on water they almost sank because Richard forgot that a new wooden hull soaked up the water. They bailed like crazy. The kids were the crew. Faye, pregnant with Ingrid, would be busy throwing up over the side of the boat with morning sickness. The wharfies on the dock called out, "And that's your crew?" when they saw Faye being sick even before they'd left the harbor. Junie followed every word of her father's. She was thirteen and the first mate. Faye wasn't much of a sailor and Nadine was vague about instructions. The boys tried but they were only ten and eight. Difficult to tie knots well at that age.

Richard almost killed Junie himself, now that she came to think of it. They'd been out overnight, sailing around the Bay of Plenty. Richard had them coasting very slowly back to the wharf at Tauranga. He realized too late that he needed help with the bowline. He called out for help, it was Junie who appeared first, he told her to go tie the bowline to the wharf. She rushed fore, grabbed the coil of rope and jumped off the boat, meaning to land on the wharf. But they were far too far away. Richard had meant to say, just throw the line onto the wharf and then step onto it once they were close enough. But Junie had blindly followed instructions and was almost run down by the boat. The water was cold and she had to be fished out and resuscitated with a hot lemon and honey drink.

Junie was fine, on the whole. She enjoyed how she'd skirted around danger. Faye was proud of her; it was just that she seemed to need patting on the back all the time. That hadn't changed.

Faye got up and dragged on another borrowed bathrobe over Junie's old nightgown. She wanted her own things, not these clothes of other people. She joined Richard over quiet bowls of porridge, sitting at the dining table, watching the sun warm the outside patio and the mosquitoes slowly dissipate. Nobody stirred in the bungalow.

After breakfast, she hand washed and hung out the borrowed bed clothes, in anticipation of them having their own things to wear that night. Richard telephoned the airport and tracked down their luggage. It had all arrived. He offered to drive there and pick it up, but Faye told him he couldn't, he wasn't insured in Junie car and he wasn't safe to drive. Richard laughed at that argument, but decided it might be best to wait. They waited, reading a week-old newspaper that reported murders, burglaries, drug-busts and Faye decided she ought to talk to Junie about moving away from this island of crime.

At eight-thirty she figured it was late enough to phone her old friend who still lived on the other side of Waikiki. Greta immediately offered to pick them up and take them to her place for lunch.

"You go on ahead," Richard insisted, "I'll go to the airport with Junie to collect the bags."

And so, Faye was out of the house before Junie even woke at nine-thirty.

She felt immediately freer, jaunting

along in Greta's clean and orderly car. They didn't have to speak much. Greta was deaf and read lips. Faye didn't want to distract her while she was driving. Somehow she felt safer with Greta's hands behind the wheel than her daughter's. They pulled up to Greta's house on the lake where she and Richard had visited often, years ago.

Greta made them cups of tea and they sat in the garden overlooking an extinct volcano. Faye asked about her boys.

"Oh, Mark is great, working for a tourism company in the city. And Jason's girlfriend is having a baby soon. I'll be a grandmother by summer!"

Faye noticed that Greta still had her piano propped up in the living room. Mark used to 'take lessons' and when he was twelve and Faye was over visiting, Greta made him play something for them. Mark was already going astray, he pleaded with his mother not to make him perform but she said, "Nonsense, Faye would love to hear you!"

The boy sat and played rubbish music that made no sense, his hands flying over the keys in a mock pretence at Mozart—duping his deaf mother—and Faye just nodded along and said, "That was wonderful." She knew he was using the lesson money for his own amusements. She didn't realize until ten years later that the boy had gotten into drugs early. The tourism company was probably his latest front for some illegal goings-on. She sighed and smiled at Greta, sharing her concerns about Nadine's daughter Sienna as some sort of recompense.

"Whenever I get her on the phone she sounds positively dopey."

"Oh, but there isn't any big drug

scene in Auckland, surely?"

"If there is, that child would've found it. She's clever. Lazy but clever. She's twenty-two now. It's such a waste, if that's what she's up to."

They spent the better part of the day talking about the old days when their kids were beautiful angels and the world didn't team with criminals. Greta's house had triple locks on every window and door and her two Dobermans were treated like kings for their vigilance against the baddies who had broken into every house on the street and even shot dead the woman at number 155.

Greta dropped her back to Junie's at around four. Faye walked into chaos. Nina baited the dog to attack Sophie, who merrily shrieked and ran around hiding in inappropriate places. Richard was nowhere to be seen. Sean neither. Junie waited for her in the Playroom, her body tense, ready to attack.

"You see? The girls haven't been anywhere all day; they've been waiting for you to get back. They wanted to show you their schools. I had to go with Dad and get all of your luggage. And now, look at them. They're in a complete frenzy out of boredom!"

"Couldn't you have done something else and... just, left a note? I would've waited on the front porch for you to get home. You didn't need to wait for me. I didn't ask you to."

Faye felt like she was the child and this person sitting there, sulking, (not unlike Yann at this moment) was her parent. She'd only gone to see her friend.

"Of course we wouldn't have done that! I didn't want to make you wait outside like some animal!" Junie stood up and stormed into the living room, "That's enough, girls! Stop tormenting Abby, Nina! Look, Mum's back now. We can go down to the bay and get ice creams."

The last thing Faye felt like doing. She sighed. Junie faced her, "What's wrong now?" she demanded.

"Nothing. Where's Richard?"

"He's taking a nap. He was exhausted after the airport trip."

"I doubt that," Faye said airily. Abby ducked out. Sophie went to run after the dog, but Junie shut the door. Nina trailed after her steps towards the bedroom.

"Gramma, why did you go away all day? We were waiting for you."

It sounded like a rehearsed line out of the mouth of her mother, something she'd rehearsed to say as soon as Faye appeared.

"I went to visit a friend, that's all. Don't you do that sometimes?"

"Yes," Nina admitted, "but we were waiting. We were supposed to go to show you our school and then go have ice cream."

"Well, there are lots of days to go see your school," Faye continued, she hated having to justify herself to a seven year old. Where did this kid learn to manipulate like this, to make adults feel so guilty? She suspected that if she had to go eat ice cream with this merry band she may strangle somebody. She ducked into the bedroom and shut the door.

"Richard?"

"Hhmph?" he was coming to, slowly. He stretched and opened his watery gray eyes and she wanted to lie down and take a long nap and forget about trying to understand, to listen between the words. Let them go eat ice cream by themselves. They managed to live without her all round the year, why bother her just because she'd come to visit?

"Junie is angry already. I told you. I

do one thing for myself and I'm suddenly the wicked witch."

Faye opened her suitcase with savage jerking movements, she rummaged through her clothes to find a fresh outfit. She'd been wearing this one through too many discussions, over several time zones. If she didn't get into clean clothes straight away she would explode. She threw on some lightweight slacks and a terry-cloth long top, in calming shades of cream and pink. She ran a comb through her hair and picked up her lipstick to reapply. She couldn't face Junie, she was too strong with her warped righteousness.

"Why didn't you tell her where I was? She could've phoned if it was so crucial to see the kids' school right that second?"

"I didn't think of that," Richard shrugged. "She seemed fine all day. The girls were videoing for some TV game and we all had lunch. The trip to the airport only took forty-five minutes. Sean had to go to work, but everyone seemed unbothered by your where-abouts."

He patted her on the shoulder and wandered out, his clothes stuck to parts of his body, wrinkled beyond redemption and Faye stood in the violet room, alone, and replaced the top on her lipstick without putting it on. Her heart thudded violently. She reached out a hand to hold onto closet door handle. She took deep breaths and closed her eyes. She knew she would have to go back out there, get in the hot, messy car and drive for an ice cream. She had no other option.

The days were a minefield of rainbow-colored emotional bombs that Faye walked into time after time. Each topic blew up in her face in a bright display of colors: red misshapen words, orange overreactions, yellow guilt, green recrimination, blue sadness, purple apologies and there was always pink resentment to top off the explosion. Junie had something to say about everything and seemed determined to make Faye relive everyone's entire past and square up every trauma, placing the blame concretely at Faye's feet. Or, that wasn't right. They were having a lovely time in Richard's version.

He reappraised every passing day's squabble as inconsequential, misremembered or just plain phooey. He wouldn't admit, of course, that Junie was on the brink of some sort of regression into infancy and needed Valium or the equivalent. He preferred to see it as Junie taking a fancy to rehashing certain moments in her life where she wasn't quite sure what her parents' motives where. He even saw it as Junie making jokes about old stories to explain to Sean how hilarious her upbringing was. But Faye wasn't buying a bit of it. This was recrimination and guilt-mongering on a scale only glimpsed in Yann up until now. Junie had taken on Yann's role. The girls played her pawns in a sickening pantomime of making Faye do everything Junie wants and pretend it's the Girls idea. Faye wasn't sleeping by the third day.

At night, lying in the stuffy room, the window not open for fear of mosquitoes and burglars, Faye replayed conversations, trying to figure out where she was falling into the traps every time.

Nadine was a favorite topic. Junie said that Faye wasn't showing her any support, was making everything harder for her, was destroying

Nadine's self-confidence and had done so, apparently, all her life. Nadine felt crushed by Faye's dominance. Ha! It was all Faye could do not to laugh. But her sarcasm was being noted; Junie pounced on any dry remark as evidence of Faye's abject lack of respect for Nadine's belief and problems.

"For Pete's sake, kids are supposed to respect their parents. I didn't realize it was the other way round."

"Of course it is. I respect my kids."

"Do you? Is that why you bribe them with chocolate and sugars all day long?"

"Leave them out of it."

It was all wrong, every road she tried to go down only ended in wanting to run out of the bungalow and flag down the nearest car, even if it contained a murderous psycho, and just be somewhere far away.

Ingrid was another subject. Faye babied her. She was the favorite.

"The poor thing almost died! They almost had to amputate her leg. It's a miracle she isn't a vegetable!"

"Oh, no, Mum, you've done it since they were kids. Ingrid had to be fussed over, Skye was the independent one and Leo was just plain ignored. You made the three kids like that. You had too many children."

"I'm not going to sit here and listen to this."

Nina sat there, at every tête-à-tête, taking notes with her eyes.

Faye reached for another Ginger Snap. She was comfort eating. She was under attack and reaching for the sugar. She was dumping double lumps of sugar in her tea. It occurred to her that her waistline felt tight.

"Well, I just want you to face up to some things. Your responsibilities.

You can't keep skipping off, moving miles away from your children, just when things get a little emotional. You hate talking about anything deep."

"Deep! Show me deep and we'll talk about it."

Faye replayed their conversations over and over every night. Surely they hadn't said all that to each other? It didn't seem possible. There was something else going on here, either Junie had joined some cult of parent-blame or there was something she wanted help with and didn't know how to bring up. There had to be a reason.

Richard would hear the two women when he came in for cookies and say a few words to soothe Junie.

"Now, now. That trip was entirely useful vis-à-vis your education at the time. We had to move from New Plymouth in order to resuscitate my career in forestry research. There was a golden opportunity to be had for all concerned."

"Really?" Junie would be assuaged for about ten minutes until Richard left the room and she'd say, "But you still decided to have more kids without even telling us!"

"Why tell you? Did I need to have your permission?"

Finally, when Junie started on a particularly twisted line of logic that Faye was replaying her own mother's guilt-inducing tricks in order to make Junie feel bad for any rebellious thought she'd ever had in her life, Faye said, "Alright, what's really going on here?"

Nina sat up taller in her chair. Eagle eyes on Junie now. Junie flared, "What are you talking about?"

"Can Nina leave the room for one iota of a second?"

"Nina, go and check how many

Likes you have on YouTube."

The girl threw daggers and stomped off, dejected. Another emotional scar born, bleeding freely. 'The time she was shunned by maternal authority figures.' Faye shut her eyes for a moment, divining what was gnawing at Junie.

"Are you pregnant?"

Her daughter sagged back into her chair and started to cry. Her aqua eyes streamed and her face grew hot and flustered. As if she'd done something wrong. Faye put her hand on her knee. Junie flinched.

"Oh, it's such a mess," Junie moaned.

"There, there. It's alright."

"With the girls, I don't know, Sean says it's a big responsibility."

"Well, it is and it isn't. It's just a baby. A little person."

"But we all grow up and it's so hard!" Junie's voice had turned to gravel. Faye realized the blame and talk of favoritism and instability and lack of attention were Junie's fears of having another child. Her two girls would feel squeezed out with a new child.

"I know you've had to take care of Sophie and Nina when it hasn't been easy with that father of theirs. You've done a good job with them, Junie. You really have. You'll do a great job with another baby. Sean's so kind. You've got a kind man there, that's all that matters. Look at your father, he'd be the last one to leave a sinking ship because of helping the rats get off safe and sound. Just having a kind man is the most important thing."

"I know, Sean's great," Junie smiled a little, wiping her face with her flowing sleeves, she poured them more tea, the liquid fell in a crooked arch, "Really, it's going to be fine.

Fine."

And that was what it took to get Junie off her back about everyone's childhood. Suddenly she was jubilant about a new baby. Happy stories reappeared. But Faye still heard the other accusations in her mind every night. And now she couldn't sleep for worry about Junie, at forty-three, having another baby. Her low blood pressure could cause complications, it would be hard on her being so much older, what would she do about work as Sean didn't really seem to work, and would Nina flip entirely?

"Have you told the girls?" Faye whispered the next day in the kitchen.

"No!" Junie said, horrified. "They'll tell their father."

"So what? Let them. What's he going to do? Turn up at the christening as the wicked fairy?"

"I'll tell them later. We're having a

nice visit with you and Dad right now."

Faye knew that it wouldn't be mentioned until the day Junie went into hospital, her daughter was a chip off the old block. Plan, then tell. It wasn't happening until it was voiced.

"There's something I need your help with," Junie confessed to her parents when she had them again in the backyard and Nina distracted with a spa bath in the Master Ensuite. It was the only way of Nina being elsewhere so the adults could discuss real topics.

"Anything to help," Richard said. Faye wished he'd waited until they heard what it was first.

Junie leaned in, "Sean and I want to go away for a few days—as a babymoon, can you take care of the girls while we're gone?"

Of course. That was their ultimate function on this earth—to care for grandchildren on a beck-and-call rota system. Never mind that Faye was barely functioning with lack of sleep or that they were in their eighties. What age did they get to retire? Faye said, "Sure, no problem." Richard looked nonplussed, hoping for a more thrilling assignment perhaps.

"As of when? We're booked to leave on the 10th, remember?"

"We'll be back by the 9th. Don't worry. We can leave tomorrow."

Faye imagined a week on their own with Sophie and Nina and a shudder passed over her. "I'd better go get a cardigan. I'm cold suddenly."

Eight

Junie and Sean had already booked tickets to fly to the remote island Kauai—apparently there was a beach there that they were dying to lie on. Called Secret Beach. Junie refused to describe it, but Faye noted that Junie's bikini was still drying on the line, unpacked. A nudist beach, then. Most likely an alternative-lifestyle, aqua-bead-necklace-attracting, cult type of place. She prayed the couple wouldn't return talking about infinite life forces achievable through tantric meditation or some such guff. Everything was packed and the babymooning couple were due to leave for a small airplane trip at dawn.

Junie hadn't told Yann she was

going away.

Faye worried about that—what if he wanted to speak to the girls' mother, she asked? Junie said to stall. The whole trip was in breach of the agreed custody rules. Junie was playing with fire here, but looked like a fourteen-year-old boy on heat. All flushed and pawing the ground ready to lie on Secret Beach.

Junie broke the news to the girls the night before, directly after Nina got her own way as to about which DVD they would watch. Sophie and Nina blanched as the reality sunk in. Faye's heart went out to them.

"But what will Dad say? And we were going to go horse riding tomorrow!" Nina's social calendar and the custody issue were her main concerns. Faye thought what a terrible thing, to be seven and so acutely aware of being split—your life being split between two warring parents, shunted back and forth like a shuttlecock, airborne, hardly allowed to touch ground before being volleyed back to Junie, then catapulted back to Yann. Week in, week out. No wonder the girl was a brat at times.

Sophie simply stared at her mother as if she was dissipating in to the twilight gone forever like Bambi's mama. Sophie swallowed hard. Heat rose to both girls' cheeks and their eyes roamed the room with desperation. Junie played it cool, Sean was conciliatory. Faye saw the parallels in her and Richard's actions upon announcing a trip.

"Don't worry, Grampa can drive you horse riding."

"If you want us all to die," Faye muttered under her breath. Sophie's shocked eyes swiveled. Faye hastily retracted. Junie glared.

Richard said, "Of course I can drive

us. I can drive us all around the island if you girls like. Day and night I can drive. I can drive with three in the car, four, or two... I can drive in the rain, but I cannot drive a train..."

Junie hands flew out to grip her father's as if that gesture would stop Richard from babbling on, making things worse. The girls' eyes were saucers now. Faye wondered if Sophie was still breathing. She seemed to have stopped and held her exhalation. Nina started to cry. Faye wasn't sure if they were crocodile tears but Junie handled it with remarkable neutrality.

"There is no need for tears," Junie said in a stern voice. Nina gulped and got up, stomping with all her might to the kitchen; she returned with a tub of chocolate and vanilla ice cream, produced a large spoon and shoveled a scoop-shaped ball into her wide mouth.

"Nina! You put that back! That's for guests!" The force of Junie's voice shocked Faye. But Nina turned her back on her mother and picked up the remote control. "Nina, you can wait until everyone's ready for the movie—or go to bed right now!" Junie's voice was losing its strident fervor; it waned in the face of Nina's cold concentration on the FBI Warnings not to infringe copyright that rolled up the screen in multiple languages.

Sophie said, "I'm going to bed. Goodbye, Mum. Goodbye, Sean." She hugged them both so hard Faye imagined bones splintering. That would be a Sophie way to throw a hammer into the trip plans—break a few ribs with her boundless love and reasonableness. Sophie was temporarily supposed to sleep on the sofa they sat on and Junie pounced on this fact.

"Nina! Sophie wants to go to bed. She'll have to sleep in your room and you'll be on the couch if you don't stop that DVD right now! Sophie is tired. She wants to sleep now!"

Nina sucked on her spoon and said, "Sophie can have my room. But only if I get your room while *you're* away."

Junie leapt on the chink in the amour, hoeing in with reverse psychology. "But Gramma and Grampa are moving into our room. Don't you want to stay in your room and after tomorrow Sophie stays in her room?"

"Then Sophie can't stay in my room tonight."

Faye motioned to Junie that she didn't want to move rooms anyway. What was the point? Truck the bags into the next room and try to sleep in another foreign cube to varied sounds? Faye knew that Junie would be glad if they didn't move. Junie nodded and sighed, a huge exaggerated sound of conciliation. Nina still had her back to the adults, unaware of these side maneuvers.

"Alright, Nina. *You* can stay in our room while we are away. And Sophie, you can stay in Nina's!" This was said like Sophie had won a holiday to some exotic continent. Sophie nodded and sloped off, hunched over in sadness. Her feet barely lifted off the ground. Dejected and weary of the circus around her? Faye wished she could read Sophie better. She seemed *depressed*. At least Nina was transparent: motivated by material treats and happiest when bullying adults. But Sophie was an enigma. Nina laughed as the heroine of the comedy snapped a heel in a New York City grate and threw a temper tantrum. Sophie was heard calling out from the bathroom, "Mom? Can you come?"

Junie swung her legs off the couch with an odd look of: You See What I Have to Deal With? calling, "I'm coming, Soph." Faye dreaded to think what needs thirteen-year-old Sophie had in a bathroom that she wanted her mother party to. Faye was never involved in her girls' bathroom life. She hadn't been asked questions and therefore assumed that all four daughters had figured things out from each other or friends. Junie returned after a few minutes. She saw Faye's hesitant smile and waved her hand, "She just wanted to tell me something."

So many secret communications, it was like living in a Morse code dugout. She felt like she'd missed being handed her secret decoder ring and that Junie held all jokers in a match of five-card stud.

"Well, I'm going to bed now," Faye

stood up. Richard gazed up at her, but didn't budge.

"I'll just go over their itinerary with Sean here, before retiring."

That was so Richard. Obsessed with travel details even when they were for other people. Faye bid them all goodnight. It was like that movie, *Ship of Fools*. They were all in their own worlds. Nina sat glued to the television, the tub of ice cream consumed entirely. Sean and Richard's heads bent over a map at the dining table. Junie's hands flew around Nina—rescuing the rejected empty carton and spoon to take to the kitchen, patting her daughter's hair and brushing it for the girl like she was a prized pet. Nina shifted in the sofa to stick her feet up nestling in Abby's belly, so her hair fell down the side of the sofa giving Junie access to its lengths. Faye's face puckered, she'd be damned if she groomed the kid every night in such a fashion. She used to roll her daughters' hair up in rags when it was absolutely critical for some play at school or the end-of-year dance, but she never sat brushing anyone's hair for them. Her kids had arms.

Faye said goodnight again, and got a mediocre response from Junie and nothing from the rest.

Her murder book held infinitely nicer characters. People who said interesting things, who danced around catastrophes and at least had semi-noble motives for their criminal acts. The people in this bungalow had the lowest motives of all: self-absorption. Faye read late into the night, hours after Richard shuffled into bed and flopped asleep. She woke at five, worried that Junie and Sean would oversleep. She nudged Richard; he fell to attention like a soldier in the trenches, ready for the

Big Push. "Go start the porridge and make enough noise to wake up Junie or they'll miss their plane," she urged. He was off in a shot.

Faye rubbed her eyes and found her glasses. She'd had perhaps three hours' sleep but her body was on full alert. She was now in charge of those two girls for a week. She was keen to guide them into shape mentally and physically—some time alone with those two might be just the thing to get them active and happy and off Ritalin and to quit being so morose. She was sure she could help.

Her murder mystery gave her some clues: give the girls worthy motivation. Her modus operandi with children was deeply psychological. Faye had studied the Maria Montessori teachings, she'd run day-care centers in New Zealand and Canada—had helped dozens of children to reach toward their potential or at least to build the Pink Tower of blocks and use an abacus.

She had deeply ingrained rules: never give children a choice of more than two things, talk to them as if they were reasonable adults, never overfeed on sugars or medicines, let them make as many small choices as possible so the big decisions were left to adults, let them do things that interested them so they didn't get bored, distract them with colorful toys. But, Faye realized that those tricks worked best with under five year olds. The distraction game was strictly for toddlers. These two were another kettle of fish.

At the dining table, Faye ate her porridge in a somber mood. Junie and Sean emerged, mute and disorientated; unaccustomed to such an early start. Junie drank two coffees in rapid succession and Faye thought of saying something about the baby, but kept her mouth shut. It wouldn't do to start an argument to send them on their holiday. Junie went and threw up the coffee anyway. Morning sickness has its uses. Sean put Richard in the picture with emergency phone numbers and reiterated road directions to the addresses of the girls' favorite places for ice cream, for horse riding, for the rollerblading park, for the beach, for their favorite junk food spots, best supermarkets full of sugar, best movie houses full of candy popcorn. Faye smiled. Richard noted everything on his notepad in his illegible script, boxy curly letters utilizing scientific shorthand that only Faye could decipher. Sean stood, in the cool dawn light, in his brown leather sandals, turquoise singlet and yellow shorts, concentrating to remember any missed information.

Junie reemerged having added a floppy hat to her simple outfit of a red sundress with white polka dots. They looked like kids off to the beach to build a sandcastle.

Junie reeled off a list of foods that the girls detested: vegetables, fruit, wholegrain bread, porridge, homemade soup and brown rice. Damn. There went Faye's cooking repertoire.

"What do they eat then?"

"Chicken nuggets, battered fish and hamburgers, stuff like that—you can make them homemade if you like, so it's not junk food."

"All week I've seen them eat lean meat and vegetables."

"But that was because I promised them ice cream and biscuits—it's just while you're here. I don't want them getting into bad habits with the ice cream though. Nina will show you how to work the deep-fryer unit. It's easy, really."

"We can't eat all that rubbish," Faye started. She looked at Junie's face and stopped. She would see about that once Junie was gone. No need to get into fisty-cuffs now. "Don't you worry, we'll be fine. I'll keep them happy."

"Good," Junie relaxed. "Oh, we have to go right now, or we'll miss the plane!"

Richard was sent as chauffeur so Junie could see what a capable driver he was. As he backed out the driveway, weaving like a snake, narrowly missing the wide drain port-side, Junie paled and a scream formed on her lips. Faye waved goodbye from the front deck. Sean reached forward to massage Junie's neck. Richard squinted and ground the car into first. Bon voyage, kiddo, Faye thought and went inside to make a cup of tea.

Sophie emerged at ten. Faye offered her a bowl of porridge sweetened with a few raisins and nuts, doused in skimmed milk with a teaspoon of sugar.

"Okay, Gramma, I'll try."

She loved it. A glass of water to go with it and the girl was happy. None of this Coco Puffs nonsense. Afterwards, Sophie said she wanted to take Abby for a walk. Faye sent them off in the direction of the neighboring park and watched the pair go down the road until the right-hand turn into the green reserve. No mishaps.

Meanwhile, Nina plonked herself at the table with exaggerated sighs and head holding. Migraine attacks in seven year olds were unlikely, but around Junie such symptoms had potential to prompt a CAT scan scare with visits to hospital specialists. Faye was always sangfroid when it came to children and sickness—her motto was don't react unless a child ran a fever.

"Aren't you feeling well, honey?" Faye asked. She felt Nina's forehead, it was as cool as a cucumber. Nina looked up with shiny gratitude in her eyes. Faye wasn't sure yet if this was a put-on, but she clucked around and sounded sympathetic, "If you're feeling well, you'll have to stay in bed all day." Nina started to nod affirmative like a battery-operated toy, "But that would be such a shame because today we were going to visit the horse riding place. Richard will have to take Sophie alone and I'll have to stay with you."

Nina started shaking her head violently, "Sophie never goes alone!"

"But, chicken, if you're unwell we can't leave Sophie with nothing to do all day. Richard can take her horse riding alone."

The head shaking increased. "I'm feeling better! I can ride horses, I'm sure!"

Obviously if Nina didn't go somewhere then Sophie didn't. Faye wasn't standing for that sort of favoritism.

"So, would you like some porridge to set you up for a nice day of riding?"

"Yes, Gramma. Please."

Another porridge convert was created.

The day passed easily with the two girls in heaven on horses, then happily munching wholegrain tuna sandwiches for lunch with apples for afters, and extra for the horses, as a simple picnic. On the way home though from the equestrian centre, Nina started up about the ice cream place. It happened to be on the route home. Glowing descriptions of waffle sugared cones, filled with three varieties of creamy gelato, topped with fresh whipped cream, raspberry jam squiggles and chocolate hail ensued from the back seat, this rapturous description made the stop sound like the most crucial action of the day for budding food critic Nina. Faye tried to introduce logic to the pair, but Sophie had jumped on the bandwagon and they both clamored to stop as if they would die of starvation before reaching home without a Super Waffle Cone. Faye turned to face the sugar-junkies, even though the movement hurt her neck to twist it 180 degrees.

"Did you enjoy the horses today?"

"Yes, Gramma!"

"And do you want to go to rollerblading tomorrow?"

"Yes, yes!!"

"Then no ice cream. We'll have a nice dinner later and it will spoil your appetite."

"Alright," Sophie said. She stared out the window, the idea easily abandoned.

"What are we having for dinner?" Nina's eyes narrowed.

"What would you like: fish or chicken?"

"Battered fish?"

"No, lightly fried."

"Chicken nuggets?"

"Yes." Faye omitted what recipe she planned on using. Nuggets would be a liberal interpretation.

"We want chicken nuggets!" Nina shrieked. Sophie was again hyped up by the sheer volume beside her and joined in with boisterous nattering.

"Fine. That's settled. We go home now."

Richard harrumphed. What, did *he* want a Super Waffle Cone? Unbelievable. He obediently cruised along at a snail's pace so as not to upset the Faye apple cart.

Later at the dinner table, Nina squealed and shoved her plate aside when Faye placed in front of her lightly browned (with soy sauce) chicken pieces cut into the shape of nuggets, with barely cooked broccoli and whipped potatoes (mashed with milk and a little nutmeg). She touched a broccoli flower and screamed as if it were doused in battery acid.

"I can't eat that, Gramma!"

The amateur dramatics commenced. Nina clutched her throat and dry retched. She presented hysterical arguments involving allergies to soy sauce and a deep-seated phobia of food that resembled trees. The mashed potato seemed to hold promise, but only if she was allowed a tub of mayonnaise to smother them under. Faye refused to budge on the mayonnaise and said, "Well, I guess we can't watch any movie tonight if we sit here waiting for you to eat all night."

"What movie can we watch?"

Faye knew that Nina wanted to watch *My Little Pony* films and some tripe called *Winx* (with an x!), but Faye would never allow a young child to watch such mind-numbing tripe. She replied with a choice of a family comedy or one of the *Ice Age* features. Nina's eyes rolled.

"That stuff is for babies. I'm going to watch YouTube."

She left the table, went for the fridge to find ice cream and spoon. She howled when she found an empty freezer. Cupboards were banged, and the pantry rattled—all junk food had been evacuated to upper cupboards and the basement freezer.

"There's nothing to eat here!"

Sophie, meanwhile, finished her plate and said, "Can I go to my room?"

"Or would you like to play a game of chess?" Richard asked.

"Alright," Sophie shrugged. The two went into the play room and set up a board. Nina stormed around the house, frenzied in her need for sugar, she hit Abby on the back flank with her Barbie wand. Abby cried and ran to sit beside Richard.

"Now that's enough." Faye stood up and moved towards Nina, unwilling to physically reprimand her—with that Barbie wand and a distinct lack of chocolate in the house it was more than possible Nina may hit her. Nina paused and stared at her grandmother, defiant, face red with fury, the wand mid-air, bottom lip trembling. "I'll reheat your food so you can have it nice and warm," Faye said and took the plate into the kitchen.

"I'm going to phone Dad!" Nina

screamed. "You can't give me broccoli! It's inhuman!"

Faye couldn't get over the kid's vocabulary. Phenomenal.

As Nina dashed for the phone, Faye paused. Getting Yann involved at this stage would not be a good idea. Nina would of course, eventually let it out of the bag that her mother was away and had left mean Gramma Faye in charge. Nina knew the weight of her threat.

"You really want to talk to your father? Aren't you hungry?"

"I'm starving! You've starved me. I need to tell him so he can bring me something decent to eat!"

Faye looked at the plate in her hands and tilted it towards Nina, standing with the wand in one hand, the phone in the other. "What would you like to add to this to make it edible, then? How about some ketchup?"

"I wanted Chicken Nuggets. *Real* ones," Nina said, her voice mean.

"How about you show me how to make them and we think of a way to cook them so they're not swimming in fat?" Faye's voice remained level, steady, not backing down completely, just easing into a lower gear.

Nina pouted, considering, weighing up perhaps how Yann would react. It might be better to keep him as an ace up the sleeve.

"I want ice cream after."

"We don't have any."

"Send Grampa to the store then."

"He's tired, Nina. I'm tired. Why don't we re-make your dinner and after you can see if you're still hungry."

"If I'm still hungry, can Grampa go to the store?"

"If he's still awake, we can ask him."

Faye hated this island, where you

couldn't even send a kid out on her bike for some exercise to buy her own blasted ice cream after dinner because of A) rapist murderers and B) bad drivers and C) the kid not knowing the way to the store. She smiled at Nina kindly though, realizing that her kid-on-a-bike fantasy belonged in another decade, not location.

They set up the deep fryer on the counter. Nina unearthed corn oil and pre-made batter mix in seconds. Faye studied the food labels and pointed out how much fat was in each.

"But it needs to be battered!" Nina stomped her foot and tossed her hair dragging strands through her plate of cold mashed potatoes.

So do you, Faye thought to herself. "I'll make a batter, I'll show you how."

She broke an egg into a bowl, added corn flour, baking powder, a little skim milk and substituted the corn oil for canola. They heated up the deep fryer and Nina tried to insist on frying the broccoli as well but Faye let that slide. She stood beside the fryer and watched Nina drop her chicken pieces into the warm oil, where they fizzled and swam in dizzy circles. Her blood pressure had risen during the battle of wills with her granddaughter and she gripped the counter's edge with urgent fingers turning numb. Her head pounded and her ears rang. Dark pinpricks danced before her eyes, her hearing rang, and she swayed slightly. Nina grabbed to steady her.

"Gramma! What is it?"

"I—I need a chair."

"Grampa!!! Sophie!! Come! Gramma's DYING!"

A chair was put beside her and Faye sank into it.

"I'll get the First Aid Kit!" Nina hollered, grabbing another chair to climb high up and find a plastic bag of band-aids.

"Now what's going on here?" Richard asked.

"I don't know!!!" Nina wailed, worried now, seeing perhaps that she'd pushed somebody who seemed tough as boots but who wasn't.

Faye panted, exhausted, her limbs shaky, her heart thrashing, calming slowly, so damned slowly. Richard patted her hand.

"It's okay now," he murmured, for everyone's benefit. Sophie peered anxiously into Faye's face. The chicken nuggets were done. They needed to come out of the oil. Faye gestured at the fryer. Sophie and Nina worked together to rescue the brown lumps, draining them in their little wire basket. The machine was switched off.

"We need to warm up Nina's food," Faye managed to say. Her vision was back, she felt stronger. She pulled her hand out of Richard's grasp. "I'm fine." She stood and breathed in and out, to show them she was fine. "Don't worry, kids," she said, smiling round at them. She took Nina's plate and put it in the oven that she'd already preheated to 100°C in anticipation of having to reheat the vegetables.

"Put it in the microwave, Gramma," Nina offered.

"No," Faye said, in a tired heavy voice, "the microwave zaps all the nutrients."

Nina cleared her plate and didn't ask for dessert. Richard beat Sophie in the first game, but then she trounced him in the replay and the decider was abandoned when Abby upset the board. Faye sat, exhausted, in front of *Ice Age 3*, with Nina's hand in hers.

Nine

Days stretched with the girls in a yo-yo effect. The breakfast swung into the day's primary activity, which Faye didn't want to participate in at all—rollerblading was too cold, horse riding was too windy, the beach was an inferno, the nature walk was fraught with bugs—but she couldn't leave Richard alone to escort the girls and she was determined to see them exercise in some form everyday.

Wednesday brought respite with a rainy day, but they made the mistake of staying in. Nina revved up Abby and Sophie into hyper maniacs—the girls ended up fighting over the dog as if she was the last bun in the world's last bakery. Then they resorted to TV and BoobTube or whatever it was called and turned into zombies demanding hot chocolate until Faye gave in. It was a scratchy, horrible day. Faye made sure they went out every day since.

Mealtimes continued to be battlefields between Faye and Nina, but Faye gained ground steadily until she had Nina eating grilled fish with strawberries for dessert and not a square of chocolate passing her cupid lips. The weekend arrived with a promised treat of one mini Waffle Cone and no arguments for a return trip.

The movie offerings continued to rile Nina and she threatened daily to call her father for less and less compelling reasons. When Yann did call Faye tried to over hear how the girls were describing things, but they went into Junie's bedroom to talk. Yann must've been busy with his own life because he hadn't made a drama out of anything, yet.

Then Junie stopped phoning.

Up until Saturday, Junie phoned everyday to see how they were doing. Nina actually gave glowing reports of activities, of Grampa's excellent driving, of Gramma's yummy sandwiches with the special mayo. Sophie never said much on the telephone but spoke about winning chess. But on Saturday they didn't get a call. Faye told Richard to phone the hotel—she hovered beside him while the girls ate their fruit salad in the next room.

"There's no answer from their hotel. It says the lines are down."

He discreetly slipped into their bedroom to listen to his transistor radio for news. Fifteen minutes later, he gestured for her to come in and hear: A tropical cyclone had hit Kauai's northern coast—where Junie and Sean had escaped to Secret

Beach, a nudist beach for hippies near Kalihiwai. Faye told them not to go somewhere so remote—the beach sat at the end of a jungle track with obscured by ironwood trees—but Junie and Sean wanted to go somewhere 'close to nature.' Well, Cyclone Hari was certainly bringing them close to nature. Faye and Richard listened to descriptions of widespread damage over the northern coast—exposed to the mighty Pacific. Phone lines damaged, destroyed property, smashed cars, winds of 150 miles per hour lashed the holiday spot, no deaths reported but injured people were having difficulty reaching the small hospital. Everywhere had battened down hatches and was incommunicado.

Junie and Sean were due back Monday. Cyclone Hari wasn't due to leave town until late Sunday afternoon. Faye's mind worked overtime to qualm the images that popped up in rapid succession—Junie harmed, Sean injured, both lying motionless, or in a small crashed airplane, or their hotel room shredded by broken glass, Junie's hands flying out to reach something safe... Faye's imagination was having a field day.

"We'll have to tell the girls something," Faye fretted.

"The simple truth can't hurt them."

"But if they tell Yann, he'll freak them out—tell them she's dead or something horrible."

Richard coughed in disagreement, "Come now, he's not that cruel."

Faye shook his head, "He only hasn't made a fuss about this situation because it's working in his favor so far. I wouldn't put it past him."

She returned to the lounge and told the girls brightly that their mom would phone tomorrow, not tonight.

"Why?" Nina immediately sensed fibbing in the room. Sophie looked alarmed.

"She's on an overnight safari and couldn't reach us earlier. We phoned the hotel, they told us all about it."

"Oh," Nina slumped. Sophie continued to stare at the television. When their father phoned, Nina must've said something about the missed call because she called for Faye in an urgent tone, "Gramma! Can you come talk to Dad?"

Faye took the phone, "Hello, Yann. How are you?"

"Don't use that tone with me, I'm not one of your toddlers to manipulate. Where exactly is Junie this evening?"

"On safari," Faye began. She wished the girls weren't lying all over the bed, eagle ears and feigning deafness.

"What part of the island?"

Damn. Faye didn't know any other parts to name. She had to say Kauai. She heard his intake of breath. "Safari, my ass, Faye! She's in the middle of that cyclone! You send the girls round to my place immediately. I'm not having you lie to them day and night about where their mother is! This is a breach of the custody arrangement."

"She's my daughter, Yann. There's no difference if the girls are here or there with you."

The girls ears pricked up, Faye could see them. High alert radar in action. 'There with you' meant it might be time to pack and go to Dad's.

"I'm not having you lie to them, I said. I know what you've been up to there, starving Nina, ignoring Sophie. Even the dog isn't being cared for. I've been tied up with a major project all week or I would've had you send them round earlier. Send them round tonight or I'm phoning my lawyer to demand sole custody!"

"How are you doing to do that on a weekend, Yann?" Faye continued smoothly.

"Don't play your tricks with me, they don't work. You consider very carefully if you can afford to mess around with this custody arrangement. You really want Junie to get home and find she's lost the girls?"

Yann yelled down the phone—Faye shut her eyes. She was going so well with the girls' eating habits. She was sure she could get them more interested in other pursuits. Sophie had been walking Abby twice daily— and thrashing Richard at chess. Nina was weaned off the biscuits and there was hope of her taking up bike riding in the afternoon now that

Richard had shown her a path through the park where they could still watch her from the bench in the middle of the reserve. There had been small niceties that were adding up into a caring between disparate generations here. The bungalow had felt cozy and (relatively) scream-free.

"Fine. I'll tell them what's going on."

"You can't do that. They're only kids, they'll be worried sick. Just send them here."

He hung up on her. Richard stood nearby, seeming to know where the conversation had gone without really hearing it.

"Girls? Your Dad really wants you to visit him—he wants you to go round tonight."

The eyes spun around again, whirling dervishes of confusion and diffused authority: things shuffled and upside down again. Sophie said nothing. Nina sulked and mumbled about a lack of chicken nuggets at her father's place.

"What do you eat there?"

"Pizza. I love pizza, but.... All the time, it's boring. And he doesn't have a big plasma screen."

Nina's shallow concerns loomed large again. Faye looked down at her hands, then found herself caught in a soft hug from Sophie, with Nina leaping in at leg-level not to miss out.

"Bye, Gramma. I love you," Sophie said.

"That's sweet, Sophie. Me too. Nina, you too."

"Me too what?" Nina demanded.

Faye turned away to finish gathering their favorite stuffed animals and pillow.

The girls were in the car with Richard reversing out the narrow driveway within half an hour. Faye waved goodbye and blew a couple of kisses from the front step. She went inside and started to pace, thinking of Junie in a vortex of wind, broken materials whipping past her, flying debris, circling her and nobody able to stop it; thinking of the girls at Yann's and wondering if the slight indent that might have been made on their behavior would be reversed by now. Thinking that she and Richard would be stuck in Hawaii if Junie wasn't home by Monday. They couldn't leave in case Yann returned the girls. Faye paced without pause.

"Sit down, Faye. You're wearing a hole in the floorboards," Richard said when he returned.

Ten

On tenderhooks... Faye was, all night. Pacing the living room floor. She knew every white-painted floorboard by four a.m. No news from Junie and Sean. Yann had been phoned and had conversed in a more civil manner, but he'd heard nothing either. Who would police ring, she wondered? An ex-husband or Sean's parents who lived in Sacremento?

Richard pondered over Sean's emergency numbers, but they were all local doctors and dentists in case the girls fell over—nothing for this situation. They watched the brief news updates. There were no deaths reported.

"Well, they wouldn't, would they?" Faye pointed out to Richard, who perched scooping ice cream into his gob. "And cut that out. I kept it safe from the girls all that time only for you to scoff the whole tub? O, give me a spoon."

On tenderhooks... as she'd been when Junie was a baby, and Nadine, because it was the late fifties and they were her first babies. Because she was scared. What if they died? What if she lost them? She was terrified all the time and not a little depressed, and if it wasn't for Richard she would have gone crazy.

And plus there was her divorce from her first marriage. The impossibility of extracting herself from a horrific union.

So, by the time they had Ingrid, Skye and Leo it was fourteen years later and being sure of what to do with babies, being confident, feeling like she was capable and could manage. The first batch of kids, it was hard. She had three under the age of three, with Faye herself barely thirty. And then they adopted Will who grew into a danger seeker.

No wonder Junie acted how she did: she felt like the new babies would end up in her lap. That her parents would die and she'd be left caring for these helpless creatures when she was only fourteen, then sixteen, then eighteen when Leo arrived. Each time Faye had another child, a wave must have crashed over Junie: another wailing creature in the house. Would her mother cope? Junie would've felt deep down that no, she wouldn't. And so in this way, both Faye and Junie were very young, unsupported mothers. Mothers in their minds. A terrifying place to be when they both had the imaginations that they did.

Junie and Sean walked through the

door at dawn.

Bedraggled, shivering, with a whopping story of getting off Kauai. Yann had made phone calls. Junie was both livid and relieved about his involvement.

Over cups of tea, their ordeal was spelled out. Faye found herself nodding asleep at the table.

"Oh, Mom, you need to get some sleep," Junie stood, gesturing madly to Sean to help.

They walked her to the room where Richard already had scarpered and lay asleep, whistling through his mouth. Faye paused in the doorway.

"I'm sorry, Junie. You had too much on your mind too young..."

"What? Nonsense. Time to rest. Look at Dad. He's in great shape, isn't he? Yann told me how he'd driven the girls all round. He's something. You both are." Junie rested her arm around Faye's shoulder and gave a tiny squeeze.

"Wake me... we need to ring and reconfirm our flights."

"Sure, I'll wake you," Junie said.

"Okay, honey."

Faye hoped that her approach had been okay. It was impossible to know if what she'd done all her life was the best approach or not. You couldn't turn back the clock and try another way. You only ever had one chance. Children weren't do-overs.

They were in the Air Canada Lounge in Oahu International. Upgraded to Auckland, again. Richard went for the free phone to call his brother who lived in Washington State. Richard only had one sibling. Maybe that's why he'd been so happy to have so many children of their own.

"Is that you, Eddie?" Richard's

voice strained as if he was on a tin can and string connection to Antarctica. People glanced his way: businessmen with their black coffee corroding stomach linings, an obscenely tanned couple, a couple of Hollywood-type girls glassy-eyed with boredom, the officious looking woman at the counter who'd stared at Richard like he was something the cat dragged in. Which, he was.

Richard laughed until he doubled over. Faye's heart tightened, watching him. *Don't collapse, don't collapse, don't.*

"Oh, well, I wouldn't say that!" he said finally. She breathed. Her ribcage slowed. When he returned, with a prune muffin and a glass of apple juice shaky in his hands, she turned her head away. It wasn't anything he did, just the obvious signs of ageing that infuriated her. The louder voice, the shaky hands, the wandering away. She was so damn mad at him for getting older. He had no idea.

"Eddie and Louella are off to the Galapagos Islands for a week. To watch the turtles mate."

"You don't say."

"Well, Faye, next kid's coming up." Richard patted her knee. She inhaled, exhaled and stared out the wide, wide windows overlooking a world of planes.

THE END

Would You Like a Sneak Peek of my new book?

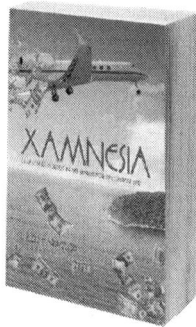

For a juicy extract of my next book, *Xamnesia: Everything I Forgot in my Search for an Unreal Life* please sign up to my mailing list at: http://eepurl.com/bkvg71. I promise never to spam you and to email only about once a month. And can unsubscribe at any time.

About Lizzie

Thank you for reading *Go See the Kids*, it was a lot of fun to write and two more books are in the works to continue Faye and Richard's trek around the globe to connect with their offspring.

I am also the author of *Triumph: Collected Stories*, fourteen interconnected stories going into the minds and hearts of girls and women. It includes two stories with Faye Ventures as narrator. Available on Amazon in paperback and Kindle.

I'm an editor and writing coach at http://www.editordeluxe.com, and my author website is http://www.lizziehbooks.com where you'll find all of my books listed.

If you enjoyed this book, consider posting a review on Amazon.com. Reviews really help readers decide to give a new author a try.

Thank you again for reading!

41810609R00102